W9-BKH-052

the knitter's handy book of Patterns

Basic Designs in Multiple Sizes & Gauges

Ann Budd

INTERWEAVE PRESS.

editor Melanie Falick
technical editor Lori Gayle
design Leigh Radford
illustration Paulette Livers
technical illustration Gayle Ford
production Paulette Livers
photography Joe Coca
photo styling Leigh Radford
proofreader Stephen Beal

Copyright ©2002 Interweave Press, Inc.
Photography copyright ©2002 Joe Coca and Interweave Press, Inc.

Interweave Press
201 East Fourth Street
Loveland, Colorado 80537-5655 USA
www.interweave.com

Printed and bound in China through Asia Pacific Offset

Library of Congress Cataloging-in-Publication Data
Budd, Ann, 1956–
    The knitter's handy book of patterns: basic designs in multiple sizes and gauges / Ann Budd
        p. cm.
ISBN 1-931499-04-7
        1. Knitting—Patterns. I. Title.

TT820 .B877 2002
746.43'2041—dc21   2001059208

10 9 8 7 6 5

contents

Introduction

Years ago I worked in a yarn shop and was often asked for "a basic mitten pattern" or "just a plain pullover." The customer might have been a new knitter and intimidated by "fancy" color or texture work, a spinner wanting to show off her beautiful handspun, or an adventurous soul looking for a "blank canvas" to use as a jumping off point for her own design. A search through pattern books and magazines usually resulted in something close to what the customer had in mind, but more often than not, the pattern was written for a different finished size or called for a different gauge. If the customer was reluctant to choose another pattern or yarn, I would sit her down to knit up a gauge swatch, get out my calculator, and adjust the existing pattern to her specifications. To many knitters, my ability to transform the "wrong" pattern into the "right" one bordered on magical.

Since I started working as an editor of *Interweave Knits*®, I've come in contact with hundreds of knitters. Talking with them has made me sure of one thing: Knitters still want basic patterns in multiple sizes and multiple gauges. In the Fall 2000 issue of *Interweave Knits*, we published The Grand Plan Mitten Chart—a basic mitten pattern in six sizes (to fit toddlers through large adults) and four gauges (for bulky, worsted, sport, and fingering yarns), for a total of twenty-four options. Our premise was that some knitters might decide to make a slew of mittens for the December gift-giving season—a grand plan that sometimes fails. Our hope was that the easy-to-follow chart form would help make that plan a happy success. The issue sold out in record time, which we took to mean that we were onto a good thing. We followed with The Grand Plan Hat Chart and The Grand Plan Vest Chart in subsequent, equally popular, issues. We then decided to step up the pace and combine these charts with similar ones for tams, gloves, socks, and crewneck sweaters to create this book. All of the projects are sized for infants or toddlers through large adults. All are written for multiple gauges to accommodate fingering weight (or finer) to bulky yarn. All can be knitted as is or can be used as blank canvases on which to incorporate your own color or texture designs.

Now, consider the possibilities that you hold in your hands—more than 350 ways to warm all of the hands, heads, feet, and bodies that you love. If that's not enough, the basics of incorporating stitch or color patterns into a design are given on page 96 and the basics of adjusting a pattern to a new gauge are given on page 97 to accommodate even more stitch gauges. I wish that I had had this book when I worked in a yarn shop—I'm delighted that you have it now.

Using the Charts in This Book

The instructions for each project in this book are presented in chart form with the sizes (from smallest to largest) in columns and the gauge (in stitches per inch) in rows. Simply find your gauge along the left margin of the chart, and follow across the row to the size you want to make. Let's say, for example, you want to make a pair of mittens for a seven-year-old at a gauge of six stitches to the inch. According to the mitten chart on page 11, you'll follow the third row of numbers (for a gauge of six stitches to the inch) and the third column of numbers (for the seven-year-old size). In this example, you'd cast on 38 stitches and work ribbing for 2½" (6.5 cm). You may find it helpful to circle or highlight all of the numbers that apply to your size and gauge (on a photocopy of the pages if you don't want to write in the book) before you begin. When there is just one set of numbers in a column, it applies to all sizes; a single set of numbers in a row applies to all gauges.

Although the charts are written for basic styles, most are accompanied by a variety of edging and/or finishing options, many of which are used in the projects photographed. Choose one of those provided, or substitute your own to further customize the design. The charts in this book do not specify particular yarns or yarn weights—it's up to you to decide which yarn you want to use, and at which gauge. The table above gives the gauges and needle sizes most commonly used with the six most popular weights of yarn. Of course, every knitter has her own style and idosyncracies that will affect her results. It is, therefore, important to use the information in this table as a guide—or starting point—not as a set of rules. Once you have chosen a yarn and a needle size, the next step is to take an accurate gauge measurement by knitting a swatch. The swatch will show you what the finished fabric will look and feel like and will determine which row of the project chart to follow.

Standard Yarn Weights, Needle Sizes, and Gauges

Yarn Weight	Needle Size	Stitches/Inch
Baby	00–2 (1.75–2.75 mm)	8–9
Fingering	0–4 (2–3.5 mm)	7
Sport	3–7 (3.25–4.5 mm)	6
Worsted	5–9 (3.75–5.5 mm)	5
Chunky	8–11 (5–8 mm)	4
Bulky	10–15 (6–10 mm)	3

Knitting Swatches and Measuring Gauge

Before starting a project, knit a swatch using the yarn, needles, and stitch pattern you plan to use. Although knitting needles come in standard sizes, these can vary slightly from manufacturer to manufacturer—a size 5 needle from one company may more closely match a size 4 or 6 needle from another. If you plan to knit in the round, then knit the swatch in the round—for many knitters there is a noticeable difference in gauge between knit stitches and purl stitches, so much so that a swatch worked back and forth in stockinette stitch (in which it's necessary to alternate rows of knitting and purling) will not measure the same as one worked in the round (in which every round is knitted).

Knit a generous swatch—at least 4" (10 cm), preferably 6" (12.5 cm), square. If you're unsure of what needle size to work with, use the size needles recommended by the yarn manufacturer (usually included on the yarn label) or on the table on page 5 as a starting point. When you are finished knitting the swatch, bind off loosely. Wash and block the swatch as you plan to wash and block the finished piece. This will allow for any shrinking or stretching that may occur in the finished piece, which could affect the final measurements. When the swatch is dry,

look at it and feel it to decide whether it's right for the project you have in mind. In some cases, you may want to knit the yarn to a different gauge than suggested. If you want a pair of mittens to be dense and water- or wind-resistant, you may want to knit at a tighter gauge than recommended; if you want a lightweight, airy scarf, you may want to knit at a looser gauge. Take the time to find the needle size that gives you the feel and look you want for the project you have in mind.

Once you have a swatch you like, it's time to measure the gauge (see right). Lay the swatch on a flat surface. Hold a ruler (not a tape measure, which can stretch and give inaccurate measurements) across the swatch and count the number of stitches in a 4" (10-cm) width (include partial stitches, if there are any). Divide this number by 4 to get the number of stitches (including partial stitches) per inch. Repeat this measurement in a number of places and take the average to allow for uneven yarn or stitches. This tells you the number of stitches you will need to knit (with the chosen yarn, needles, and stitch pattern) for each inch of width. If you measure more stitches per inch than desired, the stitches are too small and you should try again with larger needles. Conversely, if you measure too few stitches per inch, try again with smaller needles.

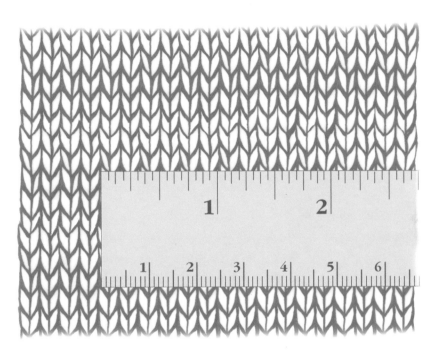

Using a ruler as a guide, count the number of stitches, including partial stitches, in a 4" (10-cm) width of knitting. In this example, the gauge (measured on stockinette stitch) is 6 stitches per inch.

mittens

basic anatomy

Most mittens fit snugly around the wrist and loosely around the four fingers. The thumb area grows out of the lower hand in a shaped gusset. In the gusset, stitches are increased at regular intervals to accommodate the added width of the thumb. Different knitting traditions specify different types of thumb gussets—the one used here is called a side-seam gusset. This type of gusset has the advantage that it fits comfortably on either hand, mimics the natural anatomy of the thumb, and doesn't interrupt the palm of the mitten—an important consideration if you want to add a stitch or color pattern.

Most mittens are worked in the round on double-pointed needles. That's the case for these mittens (and the gloves that follow). In general, the cuff is worked in a ribbed pattern for about two to three inches. At the top of the ribbing, stitches are increased in paired fashion (right- and left-leaning) to add fabric for the thumb gusset. The thumb gusset is placed along the side of the hand (hence the name "side-seam" gusset). Stitches are increased in the gusset until there are enough to accommodate the thumb circumference, at which point

All mittens shown in yarn from the Brown Sheep Company. Handpaint Originals (#HP65 peacock) at 4 stitches/inch; Nature Spun Worsted (#416 harvest) at 5 stitches/inch; Top of the Lamb Sport (#462 great grape) at 6 stitches/inch; Nature Spun Fingering (#N48 scarlet and #85 Peruvian pink) at 7 stitches/inch.

what you'll need

- **Yarn** About 75–200 (70–180 m) yards for child sizes; about 200–400 (180–365 m) yards for adult sizes. Exact amount will depend on mitten size and yarn gauge.

- **Needles** Set of 4 (or 5) double-pointed needles in size necessary to obtain desired gauge.

- **Notions** Marker (m); stitch holder or waste yarn; tapestry needle.

the gusset stitches are placed on a holder and the mitten hand is worked to the top of the fingers. Decreases for the top of the hand begin when the piece measures about even with the top of the little finger. These mittens are shaped with a spiral top—the stitches are divided into four equal segments and the decreases are worked at the boundary between segments, creating a spiral shape. When four to eight stitches remain, the working yarn is cut, then the tail is threaded through the remaining stitches, pulled tight to close the gap, and fastened off to the inside. The thumb is worked last. The held gusset stitches are placed on double-pointed needles, an extra stitch is picked up at the gap, and the thumb is worked in the round until it measures to about the middle of the thumbnail, or about ¼" to ¾" (.6 to 2 cm) less than the desired total length. The top of the thumb, much like the top of the mitten, is decreased until four to eight stitches remain, at which point the working yarn is cut and finished off as for the top of the mitten.

To make mittens following this chart, you need to choose yarn, determine your gauge (see page 6), and pick a size and match it with the finished hand circumference. Gauge runs vertically along the left side of the chart; finished hand circumference is listed horizontally across the top.

sizing

To Fit Sizes
2–4 years (4–6 years, 6–8 years, 8 years–woman's S, woman's M, woman's L/man's S, man's M, man's L)

Finished Hand Circumference
5½ (6, 6½, 7, 7½, 8, 8½, 9)"
14 (15, 16.5, 18, 19, 20.5, 21.5, 23) cm

Finished Hand Circumference

5½	6	6½	7	7½	8	8½	9"
14	15	16.5	18	19	20.5	21.5	23 cm

Cuff

CO:

4	22	24	26	28	30	32	34	36 sts.
5	28	30	32	34	38	40	42	44
6	32	36	38	42	44	46	50	54
7	38	42	44	48	52	56	58	62
8	44	48	52	56	60	64	68	72
9	50	54	58	62	66	72	76	80

Arrange sts as evenly as possible on 3 (or 4) dpn. Place marker (pm) and join. Work k1, p1 ribbing until total length measures:

1¾	2¼	2½	2½	2¾	2¾	3	3"
4.5	5.5	6.5	6.5	7	7	7.5	7.5 cm

Hand

Change to St st and inc 1 st at end of next rnd.
Total sts:

4	23	25	27	29	31	33	35	37 sts.
5	29	31	33	35	39	41	43	45
6	33	37	39	43	45	47	51	55
7	39	43	45	49	53	57	59	63
8	45	49	53	57	61	65	69	73
9	51	55	59	63	67	73	77	81

Shape thumb gusset

Knit across:

4	11	12	13	14	15	16	17	18 sts,
5	14	15	16	17	19	20	21	22
6	16	18	19	21	22	23	25	27
7	19	21	22	24	26	28	29	31
8	22	24	26	28	30	32	34	36
9	25	27	29	31	33	36	38	40

pm, M1L (see Glossary), k1, M1R, pm, knit to end—2 sts inc'd; 3 gusset sts bet markers. Knit 1 rnd even. *Inc rnd:* Knit to m, slip m, M1L, knit to next m, M1R, slip m, knit to end—2 sts inc'd.

Inc 2 sts inside gusset markers in this manner every 2 rnds (if number is zero, omit these rnds):

4	0	0	0	0	0	0	0	2 times.
5	0	0	0	0	0	0	2	0
6	0	0	0	0	0	0	2	0
7	0	0	0	0	0	0	5	2
8	0	1	1	4	1	0	5	4
9	1	4	4	4	4	2	8	4

Inc 2 sts inside gusset markers in this manner every 3 rnds (if number is zero, omit these rnds):

4	3	3	3	3	4	5	5	4 times.
5	0	2	2	2	4	5	5	7
6	2	4	4	4	6	6	6	6
7	4	6	6	6	7	7	5	8
8	6	6	6	4	7	8	6	7
9	6	5	5	5	6	9	5	6

Inc 2 sts inside gusset markers in this manner every 4 rnds (if number is zero, omit these rnds):

4	0	0	0	0	0	0	0	0 time(s).
5	3	2	2	2	1	1	0	0
6	2	1	1	1	0	1	0	1
7	1	0	0	0	0	1	0	0
8	0	0	0	0	0	1	0	0
9	0	0	0	0	0	0	0	2

Total gusset sts:

4	9	9	9	9	11	13	13	15 sts.
5	9	11	11	11	13	15	17	17
6	11	13	13	13	15	17	19	19
7	13	15	15	15	17	19	23	23
8	15	17	17	19	19	21	25	25
9	17	21	21	21	23	25	29	29

On next rnd, place gusset sts on length of yarn, remove gusset markers, use the backward loop method (see Glossary) to CO 1 st over gap left by gusset, and knit to end of rnd. Total sts:

4	23	25	27	29	31	33	35	37 sts.
5	29	31	33	35	39	41	43	45
6	33	37	39	43	45	47	51	55
7	39	43	45	49	53	57	59	63
8	45	49	53	57	61	65	69	73
9	51	55	59	63	67	73	77	81

Work even until piece measures to top of little finger or about:

1	1¼	1¼	1½	1½	1¾	1¾	2"
2.5	3.2	3.2	3.8	3.8	4.5	4.5	5 cm

less than desired total length. Stockinette stitch portion should measure about:

3	3½	4	4½	5	5½	6	6½"
7.5	9	10	11.5	12.5	14	15	16.5 cm

On next rnd, dec evenly:

4	3	1	3	1	3	1	3	1 st(s).
5	1	3	1	3	3	1	3	1
6	1	1	3	3	1	3	3	3
7	3	3	1	1	1	1	3	3
8	1	1	1	1	1	1	1	1
9	3	3	3	3	3	1	1	1

There will remain:

4	20	24	24	28	28	32	32	36 sts.
5	28	28	32	32	36	40	40	44
6	32	36	36	40	44	44	48	52
7	36	40	44	48	52	56	56	60
8	44	48	52	56	60	64	68	72
9	48	52	56	60	64	72	76	80

Shape top

Rnd 1: Rep from * to * as foll:

4	*K3	4	4	5	5	6	6	7 ,k2tog*
5	*K5	5	6	6	7	8	8	9 ,k2tog*
6	*K6	7	7	8	9	9	10	11 ,k2tog*
7	*K7	8	9	10	11	12	12	13 ,k2tog*
8	*K9	10	11	12	13	14	15	16 ,k2tog*
9	*K10	11	12	13	14	16	17	18 ,k2tog*

Rnd 2: Knit.

Dec 4 sts (working 1 less knit st bet decs) in this manner every other rnd until there remain:

4	12	16	16	16	16	16	16	20 sts.
5	12	16	16	16	20	20	20	24
6	24	28	28	28	28	20	28	28
7	28	32	32	32	32	36	36	36
8	36	40	40	44	44	44	48	48
9	36	40	40	40	44	48	52	56

Dec 4 sts in this manner every rnd until 4 or 8 sts remain.

Cut yarn, thread tail through rem sts, pull tight, and fasten to inside.

Thumb

Place held gusset sts onto 3 dpn, pick up and knit 1 st over gap, and join. Total sts:

4	10	10	10	10	12	14	14	16 sts.
5	10	12	12	12	14	16	18	18
6	12	14	14	14	16	18	20	20
7	14	16	16	16	18	20	24	24
8	16	18	18	20	20	22	26	26
9	18	22	22	22	24	26	30	30

Join and work in the rnd until thumb measures to middle of thumbnail or about (from pick-up rnd):

¾	1	1¼	1¼	1½	1¾	2	2"
2	2.5	3.2	3.2	3.8	4.5	5	5 cm

Shape top

Rnd 1:

4 [K2tog, k1 (1 1 1 2 3 3 3)] 2 times, k2tog, k2 (2 2 2 2 2 2 4).

5 [K2tog, k1 (2 2 2 3 3 4 4)] 2 times, k2tog, k2 (2 2 2 2 4 4 4).

6 [K2tog, k2 (3 3 3 3 4 5 5)] 2 times, k2tog, k2 (2 2 2 4 4 4 4).

7 [K2tog, k3 (3 3 3 4 5 6 6)] 2 times, k2tog, k2 (4 4 4 4 4 6 6).

8 [K2tog, k3 (4 4 5 5 5 7 7)] 2 times, k2tog, k4 (4 4 4 4 6 6 6).

9 [K2tog, k4 (5 5 5 6 7 8 8)] 2 times, k2tog, k4 (6 6 6 6 6 8 8).

Rnd 2: Knit.

Dec 3 sts (working 1 less knit st bet decs) in this manner every other rnd (If number is zero, omit these rnds):

4	0	0	1	1	1	2	2	2 time(s).
5	0	0	1	1	1	2	2	2
6	1	1	1	1	2	2	2	2
7	2	2	2	2	2	2	3	3
8	2	2	2	2	2	2	3	3
9	2	2	2	2	3	3	4	4

Dec 3 sts every rnd (if number is zero, omit these rnds):

4	1	1	0	0	0	0	0	1 time(s).
5	1	1	0	0	1	1	1	1
6	0	1	1	1	1	1	2	2
7	0	1	1	1	1	2	2	2
8	1	1	1	2	2	2	2	2
9	1	2	2	2	2	2	3	3

There will remain:

4	4	4	4	4	6	5	5	4 sts.
5	4	6	6	6	5	4	6	6
6	6	5	5	5	4	6	5	5
7	5	4	4	4	6	5	6	6
8	4	6	6	5	5	7	8	8
9	6	7	7	7	6	8	6	6

Cut yarn, thread tail through rem sts, pull tight, and fasten off.

Finishing

Weave in loose ends, closing gaps at base of thumb. Block.

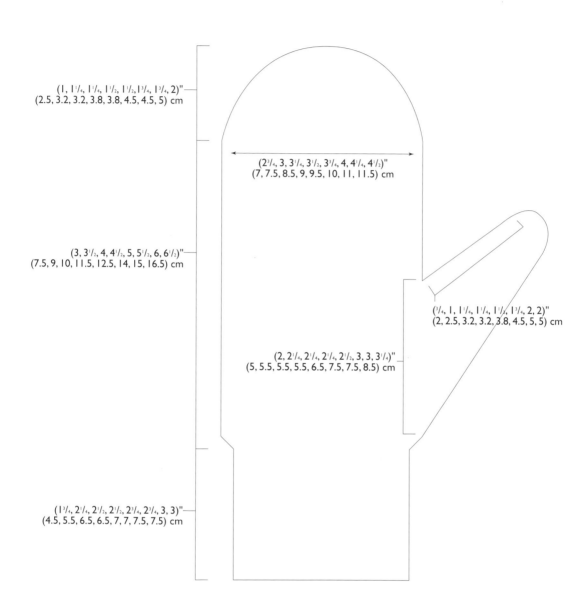

(1, 1¼, 1¼, 1½, 1½, 1¾, 1¾, 2)"
(2.5, 3.2, 3.2, 3.8, 3.8, 4.5, 4.5, 5) cm

(2¾, 3, 3¼, 3½, 3¾, 4, 4¼, 4½)"
(7, 7.5, 8.5, 9, 9.5, 10, 11, 11.5) cm

(3, 3½, 4, 4½, 5, 5½, 6, 6½)"
(7.5, 9, 10, 11.5, 12.5, 14, 15, 16.5) cm

(¾, 1, 1¼, 1¼, 1½, 1¾, 2, 2)"
(2, 2.5, 3.2, 3.2, 3.8, 4.5, 5, 5) cm

(2, 2¼, 2¼, 2¼, 2½, 3, 3, 3¼)"
(5, 5.5, 5.5, 5.5, 6.5, 7.5, 7.5, 8.5) cm

(1¾, 2¼, 2½, 2½, 2¾, 2¾, 3, 3)"
(4.5, 5.5, 6.5, 6.5, 7, 7, 7.5, 7.5) cm

measurements

quick**tips**

- For a dense, thick mitten, work the yarn at a smaller gauge (more stitches per inch) than recommended. For example, work a worsted-weight yarn at six stitches to the inch.

- For a tighter cuff, cast on ten percent fewer stitches (keeping in a multiple of four stitches), work the cuff, increasing to the required number of stitches on the last row.

- For a simple variation, work the cuff in k2, p2 ribbing, or add a rolled border by working stockinette stitch for an inch before beginning the ribbing.

- When you reach the end of a double-pointed needle, always work two or three stitches from the next needle onto the working needle. Doing so will move the boundary between needles and will help prevent a line of loose stitches between needles.

- Leave a long tail when joining yarn to work the thumb. Then use the tail to neaten the junction between the thumb and hand, and to close up any gaps.

- For a "topless" mitten, discontinue knitting when the hand measures about 1" (2.5 cm) short of where the top decreases should begin, work the edging of your choice for ½" to 1" (1.3 – 2.5 cm), then bind off all stitches in pattern.

gloves

basic anatomy

Gloves are worked like mittens (snug around the cuff with stitches added for the thumb gusset, then placed on a holder while the remainder of the hand is worked) with the exception that each finger is worked individually. For a glove to fit well, ideally, each finger should be individually measured. For circumstances when that is not practical (for example, if you're knitting gloves as a surprise gift), general measurements are provided here. The fingers are worked in succession from the little finger to the index finger. The little finger begins at the side of the hand opposite the thumb gusset, and it is worked on some back-of-the-hand stitches and some palm stitches. The remaining hand stitches are placed on a length of waste yarn or holder to be worked later. To close the gap between fingers, a stitch or two is (are) cast on over the gap between the back-of-the-hand and palm stitches. The little finger is then worked in the round until it measures to the top of the finger, at which point stitches are abruptly decreased, the yarn is cut, and the tail is drawn through the remaining stitches. Then the held palm and back-of-hand stitches are placed back on the needles and worked in the round for about ¼" (0.6 cm)—this accounts for

All gloves shown in yarn from Needful Yarns: Super (#2014 rust) at 5 stitches/inch; Extra (#2011 grape and #2991 lavender) at 6 stitches/inch; Australian Merino (#1218 red) at 7 stitches/inch.

what you'll need

- **Yarn** About 100–300 yards (90–275 m) for child sizes; about 200–400 yards (180–365 m) for adult sizes. Exact amount will depend on glove size and yarn gauge.

- **Needles** Set of 4 (or 5) double-pointed needles in size necessary to obtain desired gauge.

- **Notions** Marker (m); stitch holders or waste yarn; tapestry needle.

the fact that the little finger joins the hand at a lower point than the other fingers. The ring finger is worked next (stitches for the remaining fingers are placed back on waste yarn or holders). To create the ring finger, one or two stitches is (are) picked up from the base of the little finger and a stitch or two is cast on between the back-of-the-hand and palm stitches. The ring finger stitches are worked in the round to the top of the finger, then decreased and finished off as for the little finger. The middle, then index, fingers are worked in the same way. The thumb is worked last, but also in the same way, with stitches picked up at the gap between the thumb gusset and the hand stitches.

To make gloves following this chart, you need to choose yarn, determine your gauge (see page 6), and pick a size and match it to the finished hand circumference. Gauge runs vertically along the left side of the chart; finished hand circumference is listed horizontally across the top.

sizing

To Fit Sizes
4–6 years (6–8 years, 8 years/woman's S, woman's M, woman's L/man's S, man's M, man's L)

Finished Hand Circumference
6 (6½, 7, 7½, 8, 8½, 9)"
15 (16.5, 18, 19, 20.5, 21.5, 23) cm

Finished Hand Circumference

	6	6½	7	7½	8	8½	9"
	15	16.5	18	19	20.5	21.5	23 cm

Cuff

CO:

GAUGE

5	30	32	34	38	40	42	44 sts.
6	36	38	42	44	48	50	54
7	42	44	48	52	56	58	62
8	48	52	56	60	64	68	72
9	54	58	62	66	72	76	80

Arrange sts as evenly as possible on 3 (or 4) dpn. Place marker (pm) and join. Work k1, p1 ribbing until total length measures:

2¼	2½	2½	2¾	2¾	3	3"
5.5	6.5	6.5	7	7	7.5	7.5 cm

Hand

Change to St st and inc 1 st at end of next rnd. Total sts:

5	31	33	35	39	41	43	45 sts.
6	37	39	43	45	49	51	55
7	43	45	49	53	57	59	63
8	49	53	57	61	65	69	73
9	55	59	63	67	73	77	81

Shape thumb gusset

Knit across:

5	15	16	17	19	20	21	22 sts,
6	18	19	21	22	24	25	27
7	21	22	24	26	28	29	31
8	24	26	28	30	32	34	36
9	27	29	31	33	36	38	40

pm, MIL (see Glossary), k1, MIR, pm, knit to end—2 sts inc'd; 3 gusset sts bet markers. Knit 1 rnd even. Inc 2 sts inside gusset markers in this manner every 2 rnds (if number is zero, omit these rows) as foll:

Inc rnd: Knit to m, slip m, MIL, knit to next m, MIR, slip m, knit to end—2 sts inc'd.

5	0	0	0	0	0	2	0 time(s).
6	0	0	0	0	0	2	2
7	0	0	0	0	0	4	2
8	1	1	3	1	0	4	1
9	4	4	4	4	2	7	4

Inc 2 sts inside gusset markers in this manner every 3 rnds:

5	2	1	2	4	6	5	7 time(s).
6	4	3	4	6	7	6	4
7	6	5	6	7	8	6	8
8	6	5	4	6	9	7	9
9	5	4	5	6	9	6	8

Inc 2 sts inside gusset markers in this manner every 4 rnds (if number is zero, omit these rnds):

5	2	3	2	1	0	0	0 time(s).
6	1	2	1	0	0	0	2
7	0	1	0	0	0	0	0
8	0	1	1	1	0	0	1
9	0	1	0	0	0	0	1

Total gusset sts:

5	11	11	11	13	15	17	17 sts.
6	13	13	13	15	17	19	19
7	15	15	15	17	19	23	23
8	17	17	19	19	21	25	25
9	21	21	21	23	25	29	29

On next rnd, place gusset sts on length of yarn, remove gusset markers, use the backward loop method (see Glossary) to CO 1 st over gap, rejoin, and knit to end of rnd. Total sts:

5	31	33	35	39	41	43	45 sts.
6	37	39	43	45	49	51	55
7	43	45	49	53	57	59	63
8	49	53	57	61	65	69	73
9	55	59	63	67	73	77	81

Work even until St st section (above ribbing) measures:

2¾	3	3¼	3½	3¾	4¼	4½"
7	7.5	8.5	9	9.5	11	11.5 cm

Little Finger

On next rnd, work across:

5	4	4	4	5	5	6	6 sts,
6	5	5	6	6	6	6	7
7	5	5	6	6	7	7	8
8	6	6	7	8	8	9	9
9	7	7	8	8	9	10	10

place the following sts on a holder to be worked later:

5	24	26	28	30	32	32	34 sts,
6	28	30	32	34	38	40	42
7	34	36	38	42	44	46	48
8	38	42	44	46	50	52	56
9	42	46	48	52	56	58	62

use backward loop to CO (over gap):

5	1	1	1	1	1	1	2 st(s),
6	1	1	1	1	1	2	2
7	1	1	1	1	1	2	2
8	1	1	1	1	2	2	3
9	1	1	1	2	2	2	3

rejoin, and knit to end. Total little finger sts:

5	8	8	8	10	10	12	13 sts.
6	10	10	12	12	12	13	15
7	10	10	12	12	14	15	17
8	12	12	14	16	17	19	20
9	14	14	16	17	19	21	22

Arrange sts as evenly as possible on 3 dpn and work in the rnd until little finger measures:

1½	1½	1¾	2	2¼	2½	2¾"
3.8	3.8	4.5	5	5.5	6.5	7 cm

Dec for top

*K2tog; rep from * to end of rnd, ending k3tog if there is an odd number of sts. Rep this rnd again if 10 or more sts rem. Break yarn, thread tail through rem sts, pull tight, and fasten off.

Upper Hand

Place held sts on needles, join yarn at gap formed by little finger, pick up and knit 2 sts along CO edge at base of little finger. Total sts:

5	26	28	30	32	34	34	36 sts.
6	30	32	34	36	40	42	44
7	36	38	40	44	46	48	50
8	40	44	46	48	52	54	58
9	44	48	50	54	58	60	64

Rejoin and knit in the rnd for:

¼	¼	¼	¼	¼	½	½"
.6	.6	.6	.6	.6	1.3	1.3 cm

Ring Finger

Place first and last (on dpn):

5	5	5	5	6	6	6	6 sts.
6	6	6	6	6	7	7	8
7	6	7	7	8	8	8	9
8	7	8	8	8	9	9	10
9	8	8	9	9	10	10	11

Place rem sts on holder to work later. Use backward loop method to CO (over gap):

5	1	1	1	1	1	2	2 st(s).
6	1	1	1	1	2	2	2
7	1	1	1	1	2	2	2
8	1	1	1	2	2	2	2
9	1	1	1	2	2	2	2

Total ring finger sts:

5	11	11	11	13	13	14	14 sts.
6	13	13	13	13	16	16	18
7	13	15	15	17	18	18	20
8	15	17	17	18	20	20	22
9	17	17	19	20	22	22	24

Arrange sts as evenly as possible on 3 dpn and work in the rnd until ring finger measures:

1¾	2	2¼	2½	2¾	3	3¼"
4.5	5	5.5	6.5	7	7.5	8.5 cm

Dec and finish for top as for little finger.

Middle Finger

Place first and last (on dpn):

5	4	4	5	5	5	5	6 sts.
6	4	5	5	6	6	7	7
7	6	6	6	7	7	8	8
8	6	7	7	8	8	9	9
9	7	8	8	9	9	10	10

Pick up and knit 2 sts along CO edge of ring finger and use backward loop to CO (over gap):

5	1	1	1	1	1	2	2 st(s).
6	1	1	2	1	2	2	2
7	1	1	2	1	2	2	2
8	1	1	2	2	2	2	2
9	1	1	2	2	2	2	2

Total middle finger sts:

5	11	11	13	13	13	14	16 sts.
6	11	13	14	15	16	18	18
7	15	15	16	17	18	20	20
8	15	17	18	20	20	22	22
9	17	19	20	22	22	24	24

Arrange sts as evenly as possible on 3 dpn and work in the rnd until middle finger measures:

2	2¼	2½	2¾	3	3¼	3½"
5	5.5	6.5	7	7.5	8.5	9 cm

Dec and finish top as for little finger.

Index Finger

Place rem (on dpn):

5	8	10	10	10	12	12	12 sts,
6	10	10	12	12	14	14	14
7	12	12	14	14	16	16	16
8	14	14	16	16	18	18	20
9	14	16	16	18	20	20	22

pick up and knit:

5	1	1	1	2	2	2	3 st(s)
6	1	2	2	2	2	3	3
7	1	1	1	2	2	3	3
8	1	1	1	2	2	3	2
9	1	1	2	2	2	3	2

along CO edge at base of middle finger.

Total index finger sts:

5	9	11	11	12	14	14	15 sts.
6	11	12	14	14	16	17	17
7	13	13	15	16	18	19	19
8	15	15	17	18	20	21	22
9	15	17	18	20	22	23	24

Arrange sts as evenly as possible on 3 dpn and work in the rnd until index finger measures:

1¾	2	2¼	2½	2¾	3	3¼"
4.5	5	5.5	6.5	7	7.5	8.5 cm

Dec and finish top as for little finger.

Thumb

Place held gusset sts on dpn and pick up and knit 1 st along CO sts bet thumb and hand.

Total thumb sts:

5	12	12	12	14	16	18	18 sts.
6	14	14	14	16	18	20	20
7	16	16	16	18	20	24	24
8	18	18	20	20	22	26	26
9	22	22	22	24	26	30	30

Arrange sts as evenly as possible on 3 dpn and work in the rnd until thumb measures:

1¼	1¼	1½	1¾	2	2¼	2½"
3.2	3.2	3.8	4.5	5	5.5	6.5 cm

Dec and finish top as for little finger.

Finishing

Weave in loose ends, closing up gaps between fingers and at base of thumb. Block.

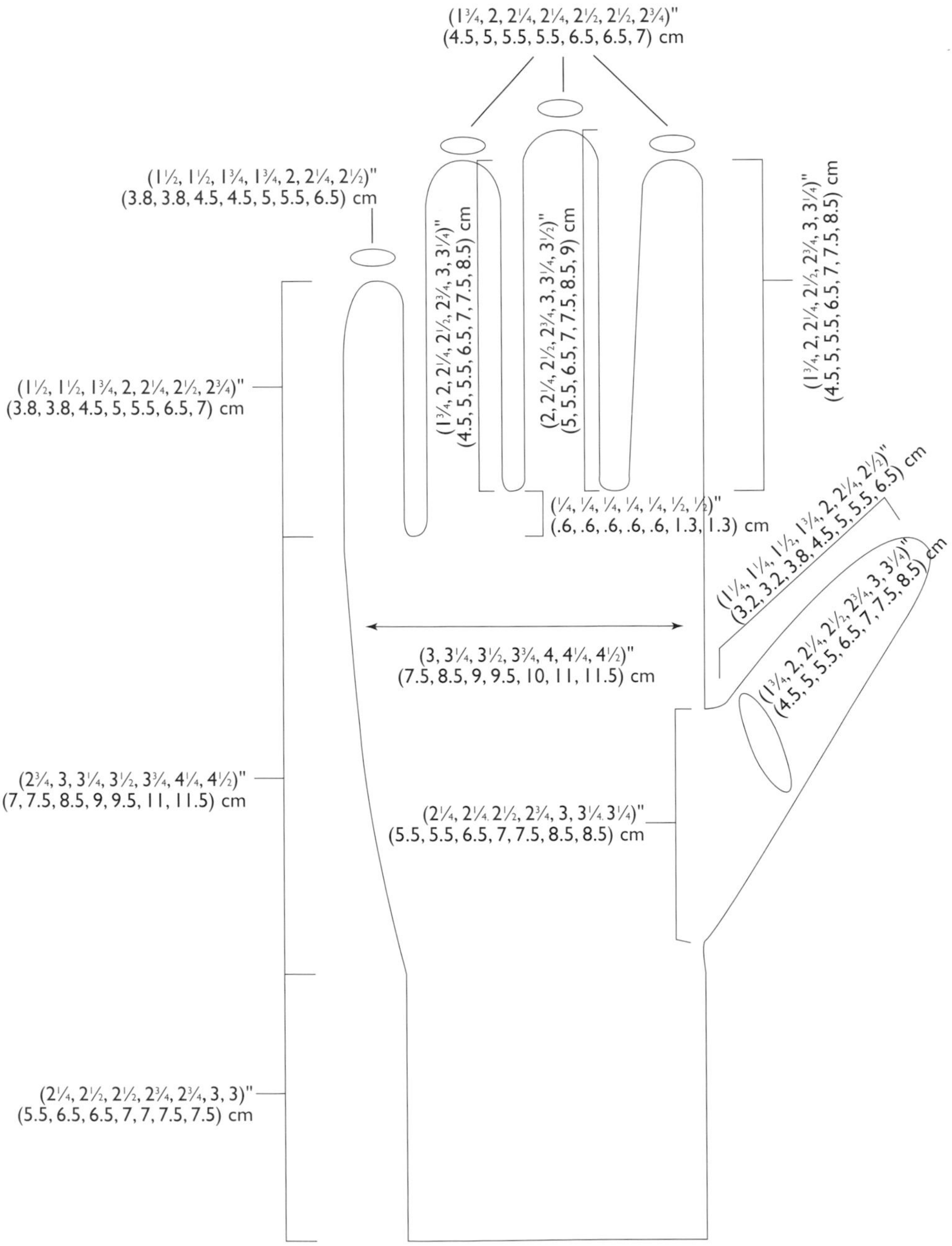
(1¾, 2, 2¼, 2¼, 2½, 2½, 2¾)"
(4.5, 5, 5.5, 5.5, 6.5, 6.5, 7) cm
(1½, 1½, 1¾, 1¾, 2, 2¼, 2½)"
(3.8, 3.8, 4.5, 4.5, 5, 5.5, 6.5) cm
(1¾, 2, 2¼, 2½; 2¾, 3, 3¼)"
(4.5, 5, 5.5, 6.5, 7, 7.5, 8.5) cm
(2, 2¼, 2½, 2¾, 3, 3¼, 3½)"
(5, 5.5, 6.5, 7, 7.5, 8.5, 9) cm
(1¾, 2, 2¼, 2½, 2¾, 3, 3¼)"
(4.5, 5, 5.5, 6.5, 7, 7.5, 8.5) cm
(1½, 1½, 1¾, 2, 2¼, 2½, 2¾)"
(3.8, 3.8, 4.5, 5, 5.5, 6.5, 7) cm
(¼, ¼, ¼, ¼, ¼, ½, ½)"
(.6, .6, .6, .6, .6, 1.3, 1.3) cm
(1¼, 1¼, 1½, 1¾, 2, 2¼, 2½)"
(3.2, 3.2, 3.8, 4.5, 5, 5.5, 6.5) cm
(1¾, 2, 2¼, 2½, 2¾, 3, 3¼)"
(4.5, 5, 5.5, 6.5, 7, 7.5, 8.5) cm
(3, 3¼, 3½, 3¾, 4, 4¼, 4½)"
(7.5, 8.5, 9, 9.5, 10, 11, 11.5) cm
(2¾, 3, 3¼, 3½, 3¾, 4¼, 4½)"
(7, 7.5, 8.5, 9, 9.5, 11, 11.5) cm
(2¼, 2¼, 2½, 2¾, 3, 3¼, 3¼)"
(5.5, 5.5, 6.5, 7, 7.5, 8.5, 8.5) cm
(2¼, 2½, 2½, 2¾, 2¾, 3, 3)"
(5.5, 6.5, 6.5, 7, 7, 7.5, 7.5) cm

measurements

quick**tips**

- For a dense, thick glove, work the yarn at a smaller gauge (more stitches per inch) than recommended. For example, work a worsted-weight yarn at six stitches to the inch.

- As you knit, poke the finished fingers into the hand to keep them out of your way.

- To help eliminate holes at the base of fingers, pick up and knit one or two more stitches than required when you begin a finger, then decrease the extra stitch or stitches on the first round of knitting.

- When joining yarn for fingers or thumb, leave a long tail that can be used later to close up any gaps or to duplicate-stitch over misshapen stitches.

- When ending fingers on a glove, break the yarn and thread the tail through the live stitches twice—doing so will fill the loops of the remaining live stitches and thus give a better finish.

- Sometimes a vertical line of loose stitches develops at the boundaries between double-pointed needles. To avoid such unsightly stitches, when you reach the end of a needle, work two or three stitches from the next needle onto the working needle.

- Finger length varies considerably from person to person. If possible, try the glove on to check finger length before decreasing for the top.

- Make a wider finger by picking up and knitting (or casting on) an extra stitch or two at the base of the finger. For a narrower finger, decrease (k2tog) extra stitches at the base of the finger.

- Make fingerless or "topless" gloves by working the fingers (and thumb) to the desired length—either below the first knuckle or between the first and second knuckles—work single rib for about ¼" to ½" (.6 to 1.3 cm), then bind off all stitches in pattern.

hats

basic anatomy

Few things are simpler to knit than hats. Worked in the round, there is little in the way of shaping. In general, they are worked from the bottom (brim) to the top (crown). Stitches are cast on to fit snugly around the head, and are worked in an edging pattern (see Hat Edgings on page 29) for ¾" (2 cm) to 3" (7.5 cm). The hat is worked straight for the desired length of the crown, then nearly all of the stitches are evenly decreased over the course of just a few rounds. The yarn is cut, the tail threaded through the remaining stitches, pulled tight, and fastened off to the inside of the hat. If desired, the top of the hat can be decorated with a tassel, pompom, I-cord topknot, or other embellishment (see Hat Toppers on page 30).

To make hats following this chart, you need to choose yarn, determine your gauge (see page 6), and pick a size and match it to the finished head circumference. Gauge runs vertically along the left side of the chart; finished head circumference is listed horizontally across the top.

All hats shown in yarn from Lane Borgosesia: KnitUSA (#3800 pink) at 4 stitches/inch; Knitaly (#1650 rust) at 5 stitches/inch; Aerobic (#41141 blue) at 6 stitches/inch; Merinos Extra Fine (#252 sage) at 7 stitches/inch.

what you'll need

- **Yarn** About 100–200 yards (90–180 m) for child sizes; about 200–300 yards (180–275 m) for adult sizes. Exact amount will depend on hat size and yarn gauge.

- **Needles** Set of 4 (or 5) double-pointed needles in size necessary to obtain desired gauge.

- **Notions** Marker (m); tapestry needle.

sizing

To Fit Sizes
preemie (0–6 months, 6–18 months, 18 months – 4 years, 4 years–adult S, adult M/L)

Finished Head Circumference
15 (16½, 18½, 20, 21, 23)"
38 (42, 47, 51, 53.5, 58.5) cm

Finished Head Circumference

	15	16½	18½	20	21	23"
	38	42	47	51	53.5	58.5 cm

Brim
CO:

GAUGE						
3	44	50	56	60	64	68 sts.
4	60	66	74	80	84	92
5	74	82	92	100	104	114
6	90	100	110	120	128	138
7	104	116	130	140	146	160
8	120	132	148	160	168	184
9	136	148	166	180	188	206

Arrange sts evenly on 3 (or 4) dpn. Place marker (pm) and join, being careful not to twist sts. Work ribbed, rolled, or hemmed edge (see Hat Edgings below and on page 29), then proceed to Crown on page 27.

Ribbed edge
Work k1, p1 rib for desired length, or about:

¾	1	1½	2	2½	3"
2	2.5	3.8	5	6.5	7.5 cm

Rolled edge
Work St st until piece measures 1¾" (4.5 cm).

Hemmed edge
Work St st until piece measures:

1¼	1½	1¾	2	2½	3"
3.2	3.8	4.5	5	6.5	7.5 cm

For a straight edge, work turning rnd by purling 1 rnd. For a picot edge, work as foll: *K2tog, yo; rep from *.

Crown

Work St st until piece measures desired length from base of ribbing or rolled edge, or from turning rnd, about:

4½	5	6¼	7¼	8¼	9"
11.5	12.5	16	18.5	21	23 cm

Work 1 rnd, dec (evenly spaced):

3	12	2	8	12	0	4 sts.
4	12	2	10	0	4	12
5	10	2	12	4	8	2
6	10	4	14	8	0	10
7	8	4	2	12	2	0
8	8	4	4	0	8	8
9	8	4	6	20	12	14

There will remain:

3	32	48	48	48	64	64 sts.
4	48	64	64	80	80	80
5	64	80	80	96	96	112
6	80	96	96	112	128	128
7	96	112	128	128	144	160
8	112	128	144	160	160	176
9	128	144	160	160	176	192

Shape top

Dec Rnd 1: *K2, k2tog; rep from *.
There will remain:

3	24	36	36	36	48	48 sts.
4	36	48	48	60	60	60
5	48	60	60	72	72	84
6	60	72	72	84	96	96
7	72	84	96	96	108	120
8	84	96	108	120	120	132
9	96	108	120	120	132	144

For gauges of 5, 6, 7, 8, and 9 sts/inch, work 1 rnd even.

Dec Rnd 2: *K1, k2tog; rep from *.
There will remain:

3	16	24	24	24	32	32 sts.
4	24	32	32	40	40	40
5	32	40	40	48	48	56
6	40	48	48	56	64	64
7	48	56	64	64	72	80
8	56	64	72	80	80	88
9	64	72	80	80	88	96

For gauges of 5, 6, 7, 8, and 9 sts/inch, work 1 rnd even.

Dec Rnds 3, 4, and 5: *K2tog; rep from *.
There will remain:

3	2	3	3	3	4	4 sts.
4	3	4	4	5	5	5
5	4	5	5	6	6	7
6	5	6	6	7	8	8
7	6	7	8	8	9	10
8	7	8	9	10	10	11
9	8	9	10	10	11	12

Finishing

See Hat Toppers on page 30 for finishing ideas. For pompom or tassel, break yarn, pull tail through sts, pull tight, and secure to inside. For I-cord topknot, work rem sts in St st in the rnd for 4" (10 cm) or desired length for topknot. Cut yarn, thread tail through rem sts, pull tight, and fasten to inside. Tie cord into overhand knot. For hemmed version, fold up hem to inside of hat and sew loosely in place. Weave in loose ends. Block.

quick**tips**

- For more rounded top shaping, work the top decreases every other round or every three rounds.

- If you don't want to knit a hat with double-pointed needles and don't mind a visible seam on the finished hat, work it back and forth in a single piece and seam the back.

- Work the inside of a hemmed edge in cotton to make it more comfortable against sensitive skin.

- To make a hat wind- and water-resistant, work the yarn at a smaller gauge (more stitches per inch) than recommended. For example, work a worsted-weight yarn at six stitches to the inch.

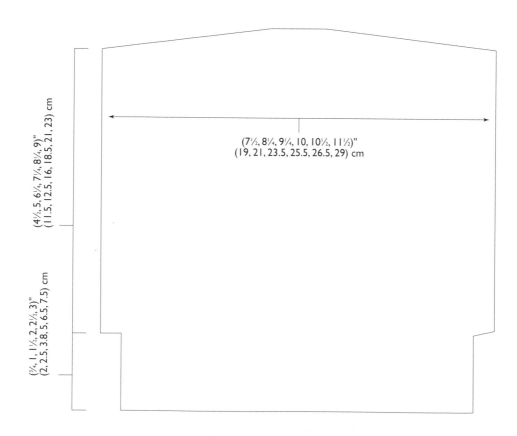

(7½, 8¼, 9¼, 10, 10½, 11½)"
(19, 21, 23.5, 25.5, 26.5, 29) cm

(4½, 5, 6¼, 7¼, 8¼, 9)"
(11.5, 12.5, 16, 18.5, 21, 23) cm

(¾, 1, 1½, 2, 2½, 3)"
(2, 2.5, 3.8, 5, 6.5, 7.5) cm

personal**touches**

HAT EDGINGS

Here are some simple variations for the lower edge of a hat.

Single Rib

The most elastic of stitches, single rib is worked on an even number of stitches by alternating one knit stitch with one purl stitch.

Single Rib

Double Rib

Double rib contracts less than single rib. It requires a multiple of four stitches and is worked by alternating two knit stitches with two purl stitches.

Double Rib

Rolled Edge

A rolled edge gives a casual look to a hat, but because it adds bulk, it isn't always appropriate for thick yarn. A rolled edge can be worked on any number of stitches. Simply work stockinette stitch for desired length of roll. To control the amount of roll, work a few rounds of single or double rib after a rolled edge.

Rolled Edge

Hemmed Edge

A hemmed edge gives a clean, sharp look to a hat. It can be worked on any number of stitches and can have a scalloped or straight edge. Work stockinette stitch for the desired length of the facing (it's best to work this part on needles a size smaller than those being used for body of hat). For a picot (scalloped) edge, work a turning round as follows: *k2tog, yo; repeat from *. For a straight edge, work a turning round by purling all stitches. Work the same number of rounds as in the facing, then fold facing along turning round to inside of hat, and attach as follows: Pick up the edge of the first cast-on stitch and knit this together with the first stitch on the needle. Continue around in this manner, working the edge of the corresponding cast-on stitch together with the stitch on the needle.

Hemmed Edge

personaltouches

HAT TOPPERS

Decorate the top of your hat with one of the following embellishments.

hats

Pompom

Cut two circles of cardboard, each ½" (1.3 cm) larger than desired finished pompom width. Cut a small circle out of the center and a small wedge out of the side of each circle. Place a tie strand between the circles, hold circles together and wrap with yarn—the more wraps the thicker the pompom. Cut between the circles and knot the tie strand tightly. Place pompom between two smaller cardboard circles held together with a needle and trim the edges. Use the tie strand to attach pompom to top of hat. See illustrations for this technique in Glossary on page 106.

Tassel

Cut a piece of cardboard 4" (10 cm) wide by the desired length of tassel plus 1" (2.5 cm) for tying and trimming. Wrap yarn to desired thickness around length of cardboard. Cut a long length of yarn and tie tightly around one end of wrapped yarn. Cut yarn loops at other end. Cut another piece of yarn and wrap tightly around loops a short distance below top tie to form tassel neck. Knot securely, thread ends onto tapestry needle, and pull to center of tassel. Trim ends. Use the tie strand to form a twisted cord and attach to top of hat. See illustrations for this technique in Glossary on page 106.

Bobble

CO 1 st. Knit into front, back, front, back, front of this st—5 sts. Work these 5 sts as foll: [Purl 1 row, knit 1 row] 2 times, purl 1 row. K5 tog—1 st. Break yarn and thread tail through rem loop to fasten off. Use cast-on and bind-off tails to join bobble to top of hat.

personal**touches**

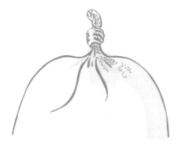

I-Cord Topknot
With dpn, work 3, 4, or 5 sts as I-cord (see Glossary) for desired length. Break yarn, thread tail through sts, and pull tight. Tie cord into an overhand knot if desired.

Corkscrew Fringe
CO desired number of sts (the more sts, the longer the fringe). On next row, (k1f&b, k1) in each st. BO all sts. Repeat for desired number of fringes, making each a different length. Use bind-off tail to join fringe to top of hat. (This topper comes from *Nicky Epstein's Knitted Embellishments*, Interweave Press, 1999.)

Crochet Loop
With crochet hook, work single crochet chain (see Glossary) for desired length. Break yarn and thread tail through loop to fasten off. Use beginning and ending tails to join crochet loop to top of hat.

tams

basic anatomy

Tams rest on the top of the head, not down around the ears. For a tam to fit well, the brim, that is, the part that hugs the head, should measure about twenty percent less than the head circumference. Brims on tams are short, measuring just ¾" to 1½" (2–3.8 cm) long. There are a variety of brim styles from which to choose (see Tam Brims on page 38). At the top of the brim, stitches are abruptly increased to give a circumference about fifty percent larger than the head circumference. Then the body of the tam is worked straight for 4" to 5" (10–12.5 cm), at which point decreases begin to shape the crown. These decreases are worked gradually at regular intervals so as to form a flat top. The instructions here are for tams with six-point decreases. In other words, the shaping at the top of the crown is distributed over six evenly spaced intervals. There are a variety of ways to work the decreases, each giving a distinct appearance (see Tam Crown Shaping on page 39). The tops of tams can be decorated with the same embellishments shown for hats—such as tassels, pompoms, I-cords, or crochet loops (see Hat Toppers on pages 30 and 31).

All tams shown in yarn from Dale of Norway: Free Style (#5651 gray) at 5 stitches/inch; Falk (#5813 light blue) at 6 stitches/inch; Daletta (#4536 fuchsia) at 7 stitches/inch; Baby Ull (#4227 red) at 8 stitches/inch.

what you'll need

- **Yarn** About 150–300 yards (140–275 m) for child sizes; about 200–500 yards (180–460 m) for adult sizes. Exact amount will depend on tam size and yarn gauge.
- **Needles** Set of 4 (or 5) double-pointed needles in size necessary to obtain desired gauge.
- **Notions** Marker (m); tapestry needle.

tams

To make tams following this chart, you need to choose yarn, determine your gauge (see page 6), and pick a size and match it to the finished head circumference. Gauge runs vertically along the left side of the chart; finished head circumference is listed horizontally across the top.

sizing

To Fit Sizes:
0–6 months (6–18 months, 18 months–4 years, 4 years–adult S, adult M, adult L)

Finished Brim Circumference
13 (15, 16, 17, 18, 19)"
33 (38, 40.5, 43, 46, 48.5) cm

Finished Brim Circumference

13	15	16	17	18	19"
33	38	40.5	43	46	48.5 cm

Brim

CO:

GAUGE						
4	52	60	64	68	72	76 sts.
5	64	72	80	84	88	92
6	76	88	96	100	104	108
7	92	104	112	116	120	128
8	104	116	128	132	140	148
9	116	132	144	152	156	164

Divide sts evenly onto 3 (or 4) dpn. Place marker (m), and join, being careful not to twist sts. Work chosen brim patt (see Tam Brims on page 38) until piece measures:

¾	¾	¾	1	1¼	1½"
2	2	2	2.5	3.2	3.8 cm

Body

Increase as foll: *K2, M1 (see Glossary); rep from *. There will be:

4	78	90	96	102	108	114 sts.
5	96	108	120	126	132	138
6	114	132	144	150	156	162
7	138	156	168	174	180	192
8	156	174	192	198	210	222
9	174	198	216	228	234	246

Work even from inc rnd until piece measures:

	3	3	3½	4	4½	5"
	7.5	7.5	9	10	11.5	12.5 cm

Crown

Choose wheel, swirl, or concentric circles for shaping (see Crown Shaping on page 39).

Wheel-Shaped Crown

Place 5 additional markers evenly spaced so that there are the following number of sts between each of 6 markers:

4	13	15	16	17	18	19 sts.
5	16	18	20	21	22	23
6	19	22	24	25	26	27
7	23	26	28	29	30	32
8	26	29	32	33	35	37
9	29	33	36	38	39	41

For subtle seam: *K2tog, work to 2 sts before m, ssk, sl m; rep from *—12 sts decreased.

For gored effect: *Ssk, work to 2 sts before m, k2tog, sl m; rep from *—12 sts decreased.

For prominent ridge: *Sl 2 sts tog kwise, k1, p2sso, work to m, sl m; rep from *—12 sts decreased. Line up decs on subsequent rnds to create wheel pattern.

Dec 12 sts as specified above every other rnd until there remain:

4	6	6	12	6	12	6 sts.
5	12	12	12	6	12	6
6	6	12	12	6	12	6
7	6	12	12	6	12	12
8	12	6	12	6	6	6
9	6	6	12	12	6	6

If 12 sts rem, *k2tog; rep from * for 1 more rnd— 6 sts rem for all sizes. Proceed to Finishing on page 36.

Swirl-Shaped Crown

Place 5 additional markers as for wheel-shaped crown.

For right-slanting swirl: *Work to 2 sts before m, k2tog, sl m; rep from *—6 sts decreased.

For left-slanting swirl: *Ssk, work to m, sl m; rep from *—6 sts decreased.

Dec 6 sts as specified above every other rnd until 6 sts rem. Proceed to Finishing on page 36.

Concentric Circles

Dec the following number of sts evenly spaced:

4	3	0	1	2	3	4 st(s).
5	1	3	0	1	2	3
6	4	2	4	0	1	2
7	3	1	3	4	0	2
8	1	4	2	3	0	2
9	4	3	1	3	4	1

There will remain:

4	75	90	95	100	105	110 sts.
5	95	105	120	125	130	135
6	110	130	140	150	155	160
7	135	155	165	170	180	190
8	155	170	190	195	210	220
9	170	195	215	225	230	245

Dec Rnd 1: *K3, k2tog; rep from *.
There will remain:

4	60	72	76	80	84	88 sts.
5	76	84	96	100	104	108
6	88	104	112	120	124	128
7	108	124	132	136	144	152
8	124	136	152	156	168	176
9	136	156	172	180	184	196

Work even for:

¾	¾	¾	¾	1	1"
2	2	2	2	2.5	2.5 cm

Dec Rnd 2: *K2, k2tog; rep from *.
There will remain:

4	45	54	57	60	63	66 sts.
5	57	63	72	75	78	81
6	66	78	84	90	93	96
7	81	93	99	102	108	114
8	93	102	114	117	126	132
9	102	117	129	135	138	147

Work even for:

½	¾	¾	¾	¾	1"
1.3	2	2	2	2	2.5 cm

Dec Rnd 3: *K1, k2tog; rep from *.
There will remain:

4	30	36	38	40	42	44 sts.
5	38	42	48	50	52	54
6	44	52	56	60	62	64
7	54	62	66	68	72	76
8	62	68	76	78	84	88
9	68	78	86	90	92	98

Work even for:

½	½	½	¾	¾	¾"
1.3	1.3	1.3	2	2	2 cm

Dec Rnd 4: *K2tog; rep from *.
There will remain:

4	15	18	19	20	21	22 sts.
5	19	21	24	25	26	27
6	22	26	28	30	31	32
7	27	31	33	34	36	38
8	31	34	38	39	42	44
9	34	39	43	45	46	49

Work even for:

¼	¼	¼	½	½	¾"
.6	.6	.6	1.3	1.3	2 cm

Dec Rnd 5: *K2tog; rep from *, end k3tog if there are an odd number of sts.
There will remain:

4	7	9	9	10	10	11 sts.
5	9	10	12	12	13	13
6	11	13	14	15	15	16
7	13	15	16	17	18	19
8	15	17	19	19	21	22
9	17	19	21	22	23	24

Dec Rnd 6: (Optional) Rep Dec Rnd 5.
There will remain:

4	3	4	4	5	5	5 sts.
5	4	5	6	6	6	6
6	5	6	7	7	7	8
7	6	7	8	8	9	9
8	7	8	9	9	10	11
9	8	9	10	11	11	12

Finishing

Cut off yarn, leaving a 10" (25.5-cm) tail. Thread tail through rem sts, pull tight, and fasten to inside. Decorate top with one of the Hat Toppers on page 30. Weave in loose ends.

Block: Cut a circle out of cardboard about 7 (8, 9, 10, 10½, 11)" (18 [20.5, 23, 25.5, 26.5, 28] cm) in diameter. Place tam over circle, spritz with tap water, and allow to air-dry.

quick**tips**

- For a firm, stable tam, use a yarn with lots of body (such as wool) or knit the yarn at a tighter gauge than recommended by the manufacturer.

- If the brim fits too loosely around the head, sew a few rows of elastic thread around the inside of the bottom edge.

- If you plan to work I-cord at the top of your tam, decrease the stitches in the crown to three or four, then work these stitches in I-cord for the desired length.

- Make a larger, floppier tam by working more rows between the increase row and first row of top decreasing.

- To make a tam wind- and water-resistant, work the yarn at a smaller gauge (more stitches per inch) than recommended. For example, work a worsted-weight yarn at six stitches to the inch.

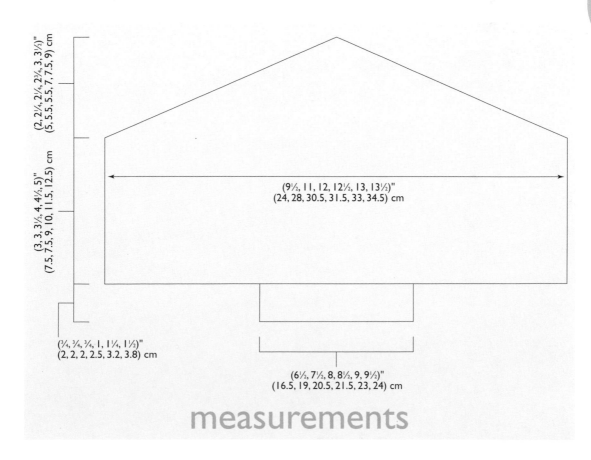

(2, 2¼, 2¼, 2¾, 3, 3½)"
(5, 5.5, 5.5, 7, 7.5, 9) cm

(3, 3, 3½, 4, 4½, 5)"
(7.5, 7.5, 9, 10, 11.5, 12.5) cm

(9½, 11, 12, 12½, 13, 13½)"
(24, 28, 30.5, 31.5, 33, 34.5) cm

(¾, ¾, ¾, 1, 1¼, 1½)"
(2, 2, 2, 2.5, 3.2, 3.8) cm

(6½, 7½, 8, 8½, 9, 9½)"
(16.5, 19, 20.5, 21.5, 23, 24) cm

measurements

tams

personal**touches**

TAM BRIMS

There are a number of brims you can choose for a tam. Here are some of the simplest.

tams

Single Rib

This type of rib has the most elasticity. It is worked on an even number of stitches by alternating one knit stitch with one purl stitch.

Single Rib

Double Rib

This type of rib has a little less elasticity than the single rib. It is worked on a multiple of four stitches by alternating two knit stitches with two purl stitches.

Double Rib

Rolled Edge

This type of edge can be worked on any number of stitches. Alone, it makes a relatively loose-fitting brim. Work stockinette stitch until piece measures about 1" (2.5 cm) or desired length when allowed to roll. For a tighter brim, follow the stockinette section with single or double rib, adjusting stitch count if necessary to accommodate pattern repeat, for 1" (2.5 cm). The stockinette-stitch section will roll up to the ribbed section.

Rolled Edge

I-Cord Band

Work six-stitch I-cord (see Glossary) until band fits snugly around head, or is about twenty percent smaller than the actual head circumference. Break yarn and join into a ring by sewing live stitches to cast-on row. With right-side facing, pick up and knit one stitch in each row of I-cord. On next row, increase evenly to desired number of body stitches.

I-Cord Band

personal**touches**

TAM CROWN SHAPING

The broad, flat shape typical of a tam crown can be achieved in a number of decorative ways. They can be especially dramatic when used with colorwork or texturework.

Wheel

The wheel shape aligns paired decreases (worked every other round) at even intervals around the crown, like the spokes on a wheel. It is typically used in multicolored designs and produces the kaleidoscopic effect associated with Fair Isle tams. Depending on the type and sequence of decreases used, the effect can be subtle to prominent. For a wide, gored effect work a right-leaning decrease (k2tog) followed by a left-leaning decrease (ssk) at each spoke. For a subtle seam, work the decreases in the opposite order—ssk followed by k2tog. For a narrow, prominent ridge, work a centered double decrease at each spoke.

Wheel

Concentric Circles

For the most inconspicuous decreases in the crown, work single decreases spread throughout entire rounds in concentric circles. Decrease about twenty-five percent of the stitches in a single round, and repeat this decrease round five or six times at ever-shorter intervals. When worked with stripes, this type of shaping produces a target pattern.

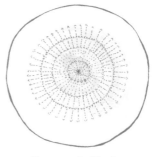

Concentric Circles

Swirl

Like the wheel pattern, the swirl shaping is achieved by working decreases at even intervals. To get the swirl shape, work single decreases every round. The direction of the swirl depends on whether left-leaning (ssk) or right-leaning (k2tog) decreases are worked. This type of shaping is ideal for solid-colored tams because the decreases make an interesting pattern on their own.

Swirl

scarves

basic anatomy

A scarf typically has a rectangular shape with the short dimension determined by the number of stitches cast on and the long dimension determined by the number of rows knitted. Inevitably, both sides of a scarf are on display, and the "wrong" side is as likely to show as the "right." For this reason, scarves are typically worked in reversible stitch patterns, such as ribbing, garter stitch, or seed stitch. These stitch patterns have the additional advantage that they lie flat, that is, the edges will not roll.

In general, there are three ways to knit a scarf: end-to-end, tail up, and neck down (see page 45). End-to-end is, by far, the most common method. To make a scarf this way, you cast on stitches at one short end, knit to the desired total length, and bind off the stitches at the other end. When the scarf is draped around the neck, the stitches are aligned right side up on one end and upside down on the other, like the scarves at right. For each of the other two methods the scarf is worked in two sections, and the stitches on each end look exactly the same, an important refinement when working with a stitch pattern

All scarves shown in yarn from GGH Muench Yarns: Lamour (#12 periwinkle) at 3 stitches/inch in Lace Rib; Soft Kid (#54 sage) at 4 stitches/inch in Mistake Rib; Merino Soft (#76 purple) at 5 stitches/inch in Diagonal Lace Rib.

what you'll need

- **Yarn** About 150–600 yards (140–550 m). Actual yarn amount will depend on scarf width and length, and yarn gauge. Textured stitch patterns will require more yarn.

- **Needles** Straight needles in size necessary to obtain desired gauge.

- **Notions** Tapestry needle; stitch holder for tail-up construction.

that is directional in nature. In the tail up method, you cast on and knit the two sides separately, then join them at the center with the three-needle bind-off or Kitchener stitch. This method is a particularly good choice for stitch patterns, such as some lace, that create an uneven or scalloped cast-on edge—the uneven edge can become a design element. For the neck-down method you begin the scarf with a provisional cast-on at the center back neck, then work each side separately to the desired length, ending with a bind-off row.

To use this chart, choose yarn and one of the stitch patterns on page 44 (or another stitch pattern of your choice), determine your gauge (see page 6), and choose a size. Gauge runs vertically along the left side of the chart; sizes are listed horizontally across the top. Use the stitch numbers on the charts as a guide; you may need to adjust them to accommodate the repeat of your chosen stitch pattern plus the addition of edge stitches to prevent curling (see Quick Tips on page 43).

Approximate Finished Size

6 x 40	10 x 56	14 x 70"
15 x 101.5	25.5 x 142	35.5 x 178 cm

End-to-End Construction

CO:

GAUGE			
3	18	30	42 sts.
4	24	40	56
5	30	50	70
6	36	60	84
7	42	70	98

Work even in chosen pattern until piece measures desired length, or about:

40	56	70"
101.5	142	178 cm

BO all sts in pattern.

Tail-Up Construction

CO:

3	18	30	42 sts.
4	24	40	56
5	30	50	70
6	36	60	84
7	42	70	98

Work even in chosen pattern until piece measures half the desired total length, or about:

20	28	35"
51	71	89 cm

Place sts on holder. Cast on and work another piece to match. Using the three-needle bind-off or Kitchener stitch (see Glossary), join the two pieces.

Neck-Down Construction

Using a provisional method (see Glossary), CO:

3	18	30	42 sts.
4	24	40	56
5	30	50	70
6	36	60	84
7	42	70	98

Work even until piece measures half the desired total length, or about:

20	28	35"
51	71	89 cm

BO all sts in pattern. Carefully remove waste yarn from provisional cast-on and place live stitches onto spare needle—there will be one less stitch than originally cast on. Increase one stitch to bring stitch count to original number. Work as for first half.

Finishing

Weave in loose ends. Block to measurements.

quicktips

- A scarf can be virtually any length or width. Adjust the numbers in this chart as desired.
- Be careful not to knit a fabric that is too dense. Scarves need to be pliable to fit comfortably around the neck. If in doubt, try larger needles.
- To ensure that a scarf will lie flat, work three to five stitches in a non-rolling pattern stitch (such as seed stitch, garter stitch, or ribbing) at each side and for three to five rows at the beginning and end.
- For a very easy scarf, choose a fabulous yarn and work in garter stitch, seed stitch, or a basic rib throughout.

A TRIO OF SIMPLE STITCH PATTERNS

The following stitch patterns were used in the scarves photographed on page 41—all of which were worked end-to-end. These are just a sampling of the hundreds of patterns appropriate for scarves. Each of these patterns combines knit and purl stitches so that both sides of the knitting are attractive.

Lace Rib (multiple of 5 sts + 2)

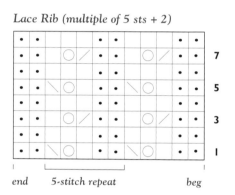

Mistake Rib (multiple of 4 sts + 3)

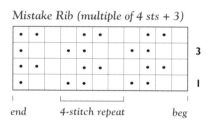

Diagonal Lace Rib (multiple of 8 sts)

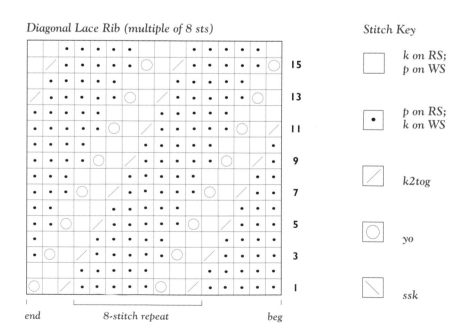

Stitch Key

☐	*k on RS;* *p on WS*
▪	*p on RS;* *k on WS*
╱	*k2tog*
◯	*yo*
╲	*ssk*

End-To-End Construction

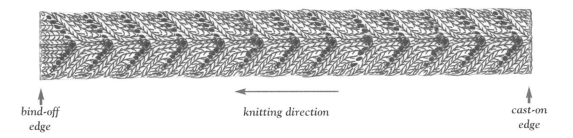

bind-off
edge

knitting direction

cast-on
edge

Tail-Up Construction

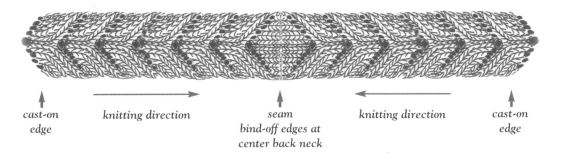

cast-on
edge

knitting direction

seam
bind-off edges at
center back neck

knitting direction

cast-on
edge

Neck-Down Construction

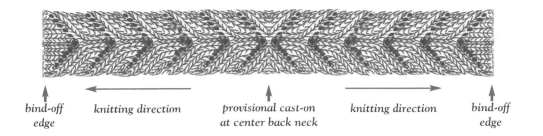

bind-off
edge

knitting direction

provisional cast-on
at center back neck

knitting direction

bind-off
edge

socks

basic anatomy

Many knitters are intimidated by the idea of making socks, thinking that they must be complicated because they involve double-pointed needles, heels, gussets, and toe shaping. In fact, socks are fun to knit. A well-fitting handknitted sock is warm and comfortable. And there's a sense of intimate luxury that comes with wearing a pair of handknitted socks—whether or not anyone else can see them.

In western countries, socks are typically worked from the leg down to the toe. (In many eastern countries, they're worked in the opposite direction—from the toe upward.) For crew socks, the size is determined by the circumference of the widest part of the foot, and the same number of stitches is used for the leg as for the foot. Stitches are cast on for the leg, joined into a circle, and worked in the round to the beginning of the heel shaping. To allow for the shape of the calf muscle, the upper leg in this pattern is worked on needles one size larger than required to get gauge, and halfway down the leg, the needles are changed to the smaller ones used to get gauge. The back of the heel, or heel flap, is worked back and forth in rows on half of the total number of stitches. There are a variety of ways to shape the heel. The method used here

All socks shown in yarn from Plymouth Yarn Company: Galway Highland Heather (#706 denim) at 6 stitches/inch; Le Fibre Nobili Merino Superfine (#4019 burgundy) at 7 stitches/inch; Filati Bertagna Gaia (#2953 pink) at 8 stitches/inch.

what you'll need

- **Yarn** About 100–300 yards (90–275 m) for child sizes; about 200–600 yards (185–550 m) for adult sizes. Exact amount will depend on sock size and yarn gauge.

- **Needles** Set of 4 (or 5) double-pointed needles in size necessary to obtain desired gauge, plus a set of needles one size larger (optional).

- **Notions** Marker (m); tapestry needle.

is easy and produces a well-fitting heel. To reinforce the back of the heel, it is worked in a pattern of slipped and knitted stitches that creates a dense fabric. At the end of the heel flap, short rows are worked to give a cup shape that hugs the heel. This is the part that stymies many new knitters; as if by magic, the odd shape emerges. After the heel is shaped, gusset stitches are picked up along the edges of the heel flap and the entire foot is worked in the round to the toes. The extra stitches picked up along the sides of the heel flap are reduced as the gusset is worked. These gusset decreases form the diagonal lines of stitches at the edges of the heel. Gusset stitches are decreased every other round until the original number of stitches remains. The foot is worked even until it measures to about the little toe. Then stitches are decreased along each side of the foot, evenly and consistently, until 8 to 12 stitches remain. These stitches are grafted together with the Kitchener stitch, producing a comfortable, rounded tip.

To make socks following the chart, you need to choose yarn, determine your gauge (see page 6), and pick a size and match it to the finished foot circumference. Gauge runs vertically along the left side of the chart; sizes are listed horizontally across the top.

sizing

To Fit Sizes
2–4 years (4–8 years, 8 years–woman's S, woman's M, woman's L, man's S, man's M, man's L)

Finished Foot Circumference
5½ (6½, 7½, 8, 8½, 9, 9½, 10)"
14 (16.5, 19, 20.5, 21.5, 23, 24, 25.5) cm

Finished Foot Circumference

5½	6½	7½	8	8½	9	9½	10"
14	16.5	19	20.5	21.5	23	24	25.5 cm

Leg

With larger dpn, CO:

GAUGE								
5	28	32	36	40	44	48	48	52 sts.
6	32	40	44	48	52	56	56	60
7	40	44	52	56	60	64	68	72
8	44	52	60	64	68	72	76	80
9	48	60	68	72	76	80	84	88

Arrange sts as evenly as possible on 3 dpn. Place marker (pm) and join, being careful not to twist sts.

Work k2, p2 ribbing until piece measures:

2¼	2¾	3¼	3½	3¾	4	4¼	4½"
5.5	7	8.5	9	9.5	10	11	11.5 cm

Change to smaller dpn and cont in established rib until total length measures:

4½	5½	6½	7	7½	8	8½	9"
11.5	14	16.5	18	19	20.5	21.5	23 cm

Heel

Knit across:

5	7	8	9	10	11	12	12	13 sts,
6	8	10	11	12	13	14	14	15
7	10	11	13	14	15	16	17	18
8	11	13	15	16	17	18	19	20
9	12	15	17	18	19	20	21	22

turn work, and purl across:

5	14	16	18	20	22	24	24	26 sts.
6	16	20	22	24	26	28	28	30
7	20	22	26	28	30	32	34	36
8	22	26	30	32	34	36	38	40
9	24	30	34	36	38	40	42	44

Place rem sts on spare needle or holder to work later for instep.

Total heel sts:

5	14	16	18	20	22	24	24	26 sts.
6	16	20	22	24	26	28	28	30
7	20	22	26	28	30	32	34	36
8	22	26	30	32	34	36	38	40
9	24	30	34	36	38	40	42	44

Heel flap

Work back and forth on heel sts as foll:

Row 1: (RS) *Sl 1 pwise with yarn in back (wyb), k1; rep from *.

Row 2: Sl 1 pwise with yarn in front (wyf), purl to end.

Rep Rows 1 and 2 until the following number of rows have been worked:

5	14	16	18	20	22	24	24	26 rows.
6	16	20	22	24	26	28	28	30
7	20	22	26	28	30	32	34	36
8	22	26	30	32	34	36	38	40
9	24	30	34	36	38	40	42	44

There will be the following number of chain selvedge sts:

5	7	8	9	10	11	12	12	13 sts.
6	8	10	11	12	13	14	14	15
7	10	11	13	14	15	16	17	18
8	11	13	15	16	17	18	19	20
9	12	15	17	18	19	20	21	22

Turn heel

Row 1: (RS) Knit across:

5	9	10	11	12	13	14	14	15 sts,
6	10	12	13	14	15	16	16	17
7	12	13	15	16	17	18	19	20
8	13	15	17	18	19	20	21	22
9	14	17	19	20	21	22	23	24

ssk, k1, turn work.

Row 2: Sl 1 pwise, p5, p2tog, p1, turn.

Row 3: Sl 1 pwise, knit to 1 st before gap, ssk (1 st from each side of gap), k1, turn.

Row 4: Sl 1 pwise, purl to 1 st before gap, p2tog (1 st from each side of gap), p1, turn.

socks

Rep Rows 3 and 4 until all heel sts have been worked, ending with a WS row, and ending p2tog if there are not enough sts to end p2tog, p1. There will remain:

5	10	10	12	12	14	14	14	16 sts.
6	10	12	14	14	16	16	16	18
7	12	14	16	16	18	18	20	20
8	14	16	18	18	20	20	22	22
9	14	18	20	20	22	22	24	24

Heel gusset

Knit across all heel sts and, with same dpn (needle 1), pick up and knit:

5	7	8	9	10	11	12	12	13 sts
6	8	10	11	12	13	14	14	15
7	10	11	13	14	15	16	17	18
8	11	13	15	16	17	18	19	20
9	12	15	17	18	19	20	21	22

along selvedge edge of heel flap; with another dpn (needle 2) work across held instep sts; with another dpn (needle 3), pick up and knit:

5	7	8	9	10	11	12	12	13 sts
6	8	10	11	12	13	14	14	15
7	10	11	13	14	15	16	17	18
8	11	13	15	16	17	18	19	20
9	12	15	17	18	19	20	21	22

along other side of heel, and knit across half of heel sts. Total sts:

5	38	42	48	52	58	62	62	68 sts.
6	42	52	58	62	68	72	72	78
7	52	58	68	72	78	82	88	92
8	58	68	78	82	88	92	98	102
9	62	78	88	92	98	102	108	112

Rnd now begins at center back heel.

Rnd 1: Knit to last 3 sts on needle 1, k2tog, k1; knit across all instep sts on needle 2; at beg of needle 3, k1, ssk, knit to end—2 gusset sts dec'd.

Rnd 2: Knit.

Rep Rnds 1 and 2 until there remain:

5	28	32	36	40	44	48	48	52 sts.
6	32	40	44	48	52	56	56	60
7	40	44	52	56	60	64	68	72
8	44	52	60	64	68	72	76	80
9	48	60	68	72	76	80	84	88

Foot

Work even in St st until piece measures from back of heel:

4½	5½	6½	7½	8	8	8½	9"
11.5	14	16.5	19	20.5	20.5	21.5	23 cm

or about:

1¼	1½	1¾	2	2	2¼	2¼	2½"
3.2	3.8	4.5	5	5	5.5	5.5	6.5 cm

less than desired total foot length.

Toe

Rnd 1: On needle 1, knit to last 3 sts, k2tog, k1; on needle 2, k1, ssk, work to last 3 sts, k2tog, k1; on needle 3, k1, ssk, knit to end—4 sts dec'd.

Rnd 2: Knit.

Rep Rnds 1 and 2 until there remain:

5	16	16	16	20	20	24	24	28 sts.
6	16	20	20	24	24	28	28	32
7	20	20	24	28	28	32	36	36
8	20	24	28	32	36	36	40	40
9	24	28	32	36	40	40	44	44

Rep Rnd 1 only until there remain:

5	4	8	8	8	8	8	8	8 sts.
6	8	8	8	8	8	8	8	8
7	8	8	8	8	8	8	8	8
8	8	8	8	12	12	12	12	12
9	12	12	12	12	12	12	12	12

socks

Knit sts from needle 1 onto needle 3—there will be the same number of sts on each of 2 needles. Cut yarn leaving an 18" (46-cm) tail. Using the Kitchener st (see Glossary), graft rem sts tog.

Finishing

Weave in loose ends. Block under a damp towel or on sock blockers.

quick**tips**

- To give the heels and toes of your socks longer life, work a strand of sewing thread with the yarn while working the heel flap, turning the heel, and working the toe shaping.

- To tighten the join between the heel flap and gusset, pick up stitches through the back loop of the chain edge stitches (in effect, twisting the stitches) along the heel flap (see Glossary).

- To help close potential gaps at the base of gussets, pick up an extra stitch at the base of each gusset (between the heel flap and instep stitches). Work these stitches together with the edge instep stitches on the next row.

- For a dense, warm sock, work the yarn at a smaller gauge (more stitches per inch) than recommended. For example, work a worsted-weight yarn at 6 stitches to the inch.

- To avoid casting on too tightly, cast on using two needles held together or onto needles a couple of sizes larger than you plan to use. Or, use a very elastic method, such as the Norwegian cast-on (see Glossary).

- Sometimes a vertical line of loose stitches develops at the boundaries between double-pointed needles. To avoid such unsightly stitches, when you reach the end of a needle, work two or three stitches from the next needle onto the working needle.

- For a simple variation, extend the leg pattern along the instep stitches (but not the heel or sole stitches) to where the toe shaping begins.

SOCKS

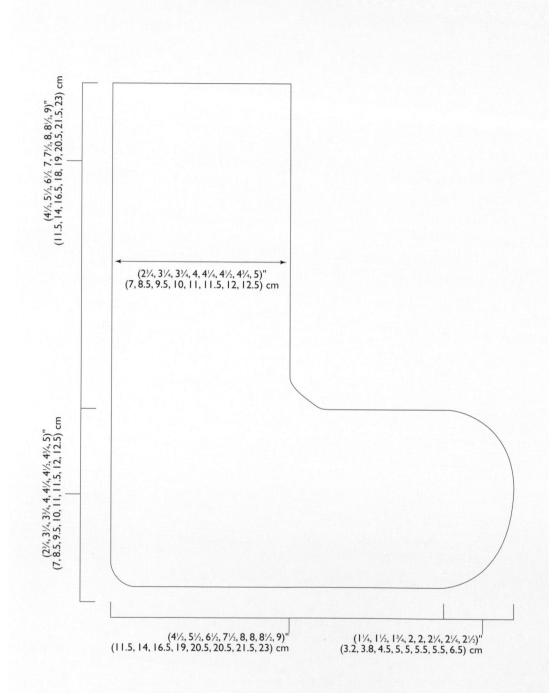

(4½, 5½, 6½, 7, 7½, 8, 8½, 9)"
(11.5, 14, 16.5, 18, 19, 20.5, 21.5, 23) cm

(2¾, 3¼, 3¾, 4, 4¼, 4½, 4¾, 5)"
(7, 8.5, 9.5, 10, 11, 11.5, 12, 12.5) cm

(2¾, 3¼, 3¾, 4, 4¼, 4½, 4¾, 5)"
(7, 8.5, 9.5, 10, 11, 11.5, 12, 12.5) cm

(4½, 5½, 6½, 7½, 8, 8, 8½, 9)"
(11.5, 14, 16.5, 19, 20.5, 20.5, 21.5, 23) cm

(1¼, 1½, 1¾, 2, 2, 2¼, 2¼, 2½)"
(3.2, 3.8, 4.5, 5, 5, 5.5, 5.5, 6.5) cm

measurements

personal**touches**

SOCK LEGS

Many socks feature ribbing at the top of the leg or down the entire length of the leg. The ribbing helps hold the socks on and has variable give that allows it to fit snugly on a variety of leg shapes. Rolled and picot edges provide more unique and decorative looks and a looser fit.

Single Rib

The most elastic of stitches, single rib is worked on an even number of stitches by alternating one knit stitch with one purl stitch.

Single Rib

Double Rib

Double rib contracts less than single rib, and may be more comfortable for those with larger legs. It requires a multiple of four stitches and is worked by alternating two knit stitches with two purl stitches.

Double Rib

Rolled Edge

A rolled edge gives a casual look to a sock, but because it adds bulk, is not commonly used with thick yarn. A rolled edge can be worked on any number of stitches. Simply work stockinette stitch for desired length of roll. To control the amount of roll, work a few rounds of single or double rib between the rolled edging and the sock leg.

Picot Edge

This pretty edge adds a dressy look to socks. It is worked on an even number of stitches. Work stockinette stitch for the desired length of the facing (to avoid excess bulk, work this part on needles a size smaller than those being used for the rest of the sock), work a turning round as follows: *k2tog, yo; repeat from *. Work the same number of rounds as in the facing, then fold facing along turning round to inside of sock, and attach as follows: Pick up the edge of the first cast-on stitch and knit this together with the first stitch on the needle. Continue around in this manner, working the edge of the corresponding cast-on stitch together with the stitch on the needle.

Rolled Edge

Picot Edge

SOCKS

53

vests

basic anatomy

Vests are simply sweaters without sleeves. In general, a vest is knitted upward from the hips or waist to the neck, with a few stitches removed at the armholes to reduce the width of the chest and upper back. For a pullover version, the front is worked the same as the back, but extra stitches are decreased at the center front to shape the neck. For a cardigan version, the front is worked in two pieces—each with half the number of stitches used for the back. The pieces are blocked, sewn together, and the arm, neck, and center front edges are finished with the desired edging treatment. This vest features a V-neck. To make a crew neck, follow the front neck shaping instructions for the sweater (see page 72).

To make a vest following this chart, you need to choose yarn, determine your gauge (see page 6), and pick a size and match it to the finished bust/chest circumference. Gauge runs vertically along the left side of the chart; finished bust/chest circumference is listed horizontally across the top. The child chart begins on page 56; the adult chart begins on page 60. Schematics for all sizes begin on page 66.

All vests shown in yarn from Baabajoes Wool Company: NZ WoolPak 8-Ply (#30 mountain green) at 6 stitches/inch; NZ WoolPak 10-Ply (#33 bluebell) at 5 stitches/inch; NZ WoolPak 12-Ply (#35 aubergine) 4 stitches/inch.

what you'll need

- **Yarn** About 600–1,000 yards (550–925 m) for child sizes; about 900–2,000 yards (825–1,825 m) for adult sizes. Exact amount will depend on vest size and yarn gauge.

- **Needles** Straight needles in size necessary to obtain the desired gauge.

- **Notions** Stitch holder; tapestry needle; buttons for cardigan: 4 for child, 5 or 6 for adult.

sizing

To Fit Sizes
2–4 years (4–6 years, 6–8 years, 8–10 years, 10–12 years)

Finished Chest Circumference
26 (28, 30, 32, 34)"
66 (71, 76, 81.5, 86.5) cm

Finished Chest Circumference

26	28	30	32	34"
66	71	76	81.5	86.5 cm

Pullover Back
CO:

GAUGE					
3	38	42	44	48	50 sts.
4	52	56	60	64	68
5	64	70	74	80	86
6	78	84	90	96	102
7	90	98	106	112	120

Work edging of choice (see page 70), then cont even until piece measures desired length from beg, or about:

7¾	8½	10½	12	13"
19.5	21.5	26.5	30.5	33 cm

Shape armholes
At beg of next 2 rows BO:

3	2	2	2	2	2 sts.
4	3	3	3	3	3
5	4	4	4	4	4
6	5	5	5	5	5
7	5	5	5	5	6

At beg of foll 2 rows BO:

3	1	2	2	2	2 st(s).
4	3	3	3	3	3
5	3	3	3	3	3
6	4	4	4	4	4
7	4	4	4	4	4

Dec 1 st each end of needle every RS row:

3	1	1	1	2	2 time(s).
4	1	1	1	2	2
5	1	1	1	2	2
6	1	1	1	2	2
7	2	2	2	3	3

There will remain:

3	30	32	34	36	38 sts.
4	38	42	46	48	52
5	48	54	58	62	68
6	58	64	70	74	80
7	68	76	84	88	94

Cont even until armholes measure:

5½	6	7	7½	8"
14	15	18	19	20.5 cm

Shape shoulders

At beg of next 2 rows BO:

3	4	4	4	4	5 sts.
4	5	5	6	6	7
5	6	7	7	8	6
6	7	6	6	7	8
7	6	7	7	8	9

At beg of foll 2 rows BO:

3	4	4	4	5	5 sts.
4	4	5	5	6	7
5	6	7	7	8	6
6	7	5	6	6	7
7	5	6	7	8	8

At beg of foll 2 rows BO (if number is zero, omit these rows):

3	0	0	0	0	0 sts.
4	0	0	0	0	0
5	0	0	0	0	6
6	0	5	5	6	7
7	5	6	7	7	8

BO rem sts for back neck:

3	14	16	18	18	18 sts.
4	20	22	24	24	24
5	24	26	30	30	32
6	30	32	36	36	36
7	36	38	42	42	44

Pullover Front

Work as for back until armholes measure:

½	¾	1	1½	2"
1.3	2	2.5	3.8	5 cm

Shape V-neck

With RS facing, work to center of row. Turn, and work these sts only to shoulder (place rem sts on a holder to work later). Cont to work armhole shaping as for back, if necessary, and *at the same time*, dec 1 st at neck edge every RS row:

3	7	8	9	9	9 times.
4	10	11	11	11	11
5	11	12	12	12	13
6	13	14	15	15	15
7	16	16	18	18	19

Then dec 1 st at neck edge every 4 rows (if number is zero, omit these rows):

3	0	0	0	0	0 time(s).
4	0	0	1	1	1
5	1	1	3	3	3
6	2	2	3	3	3
7	2	3	3	3	3

There will remain:

3	8	8	8	9	10 sts.
4	9	10	11	12	14
5	12	14	14	16	18
6	14	16	17	19	22
7	16	19	21	23	25

Work even until armhole measures same as back to shoulder. Shape shoulder as for back. Rejoin yarn at neck edge of held sts and work as for first half, reversing neck and shoulder shaping.

Finishing

Block pieces to measurements. With yarn threaded on a tapestry needle, sew one shoulder seam.

Neckband: With RS facing and beg at other shoulder, pick up and knit 1 st for each BO st along back neck, pick up and knit about 3 sts for every 4 rows down to center front neck, M1 (see Glossary) at base of V shaping, pick up and knit about 3 sts for every 4 rows along front to shoulder. Adjust sts if necessary to achieve a full multiple of the edging pattern you've chosen. Work in chosen pattern until neckband measures ¾" (2 cm), or desired length, working a double decrease (sl 2 tog kwise, k1, p2sso) at center point of V every other row. BO all sts in patt. Sew rem shoulder seam.

Armbands: With RS facing and beg at underarm, pick up and knit 3 sts for every 4 rows around armhole, adjusting the number of sts if necessary to achieve a full multiple of the edging pattern you've chosen. Work in chosen pattern until armband measures ¾" (2 cm), or desired length. BO all sts in patt. Sew side seams. Weave in loose ends. Block again, if desired.

Cardigan Back

Work as for pullover version.

Cardigan Left Front

CO:

3	20	21	23	24	26 sts.
4	26	28	30	32	34
5	32	35	37	40	43
6	39	42	45	48	51
7	45	49	53	56	60

Work edging of choice (see page 70), then cont even until piece measures same as back to armhole.

Shape armhole

At beg of next RS row BO:

3	2	2	2	2	3 sts.
4	3	3	3	3	3
5	4	4	4	4	4
6	5	5	5	5	5
7	5	5	5	5	6

At beg of next RS row BO:

3	2	2	2	2	2 sts.
4	3	3	3	3	3
5	3	3	3	3	3
6	4	4	4	4	4
7	4	4	4	4	4

Dec 1 st at armhole edge (beg of every RS row):

3	1	1	2	2	2 time(s).
4	1	1	1	2	2
5	1	1	1	2	2
6	1	1	1	2	2
7	2	2	2	3	3

There will remain:

3	15	16	17	18	19 sts.
4	19	21	23	24	26
5	24	27	29	31	34
6	29	32	35	37	40
7	34	38	42	44	47

Cont even until armhole measures:

½	¾	1	1½	2"
1.3	2	2.5	3.8	5 cm

Shape V-neck

Dec 1 st at neck edge (end of every RS row):

3	7	8	9	9	9 times
4	10	11	11	11	11
5	11	12	12	12	13
6	13	14	15	15	15
7	16	16	18	18	19

Vests

Then dec 1 st at neck edge (end of RS row) every 4 rows (if number is zero, omit these rows):

3	0	0	0	0	0 time(s).
4	0	0	1	1	1
5	1	1	3	3	3
6	2	2	3	3	3
7	2	3	3	3	3

There will remain:

3	8	8	8	9	10 sts.
4	9	10	11	12	14
5	12	14	14	16	18
6	14	16	17	19	22
7	16	19	21	23	25

Cont even until armhole measures:

5½	6	7	7½	8"
14	15	18	19	20.5 cm

Shape shoulder

At beg of next RS row (armhole edge) BO:

3	4	4	4	4	5 sts.
4	5	5	6	6	7
5	6	7	7	8	6
6	7	6	6	7	8
7	6	7	7	8	9

At beg of foll RS row BO:

3	4	4	4	5	5 sts.
4	4	5	5	6	7
5	6	7	7	8	6
6	7	5	6	6	7
7	5	6	7	8	8

At beg of foll RS row BO (if number is zero, omit these rows):

3	0	0	0	0	0 sts.
4	0	0	0	0	0
5	0	0	0	0	6
6	0	5	5	6	7
7	5	6	7	7	8

Cardigan Right Front

Work as for left front, but reverse shaping (i.e., BO for armhole and shoulder at beg of WS rows; shape neck at beg of RS rows).

Finishing

Block pieces to measurements. With yarn threaded on a tapestry needle, sew shoulder seams. On left front (for females) or right front (for males), mark placement of 4 buttons, one ½" (1.3 cm) up from CO edge, one at beg of neck shaping, and the others evenly spaced in between. *Neck/front band:* With RS facing and beg at lower right front edge, pick up and knit about 3 sts for every 4 rows along front to shoulder, pick up and knit 1 st for each BO st along back neck, pick up and knit about 3 sts for every 4 rows down left front. Adjust sts if necessary to achieve a full multiple of the edging pattern you've chosen. Work in chosen pattern until band measures ¾" (2 cm), working one-row buttonholes (see Glossary) opposite markers (on right front for females; left front for males) when band measures between ¼" and ½" (0.6 cm and 1.3 cm). BO all sts in patt.
Armbands: Work as for pullover. Weave in loose ends. Sew buttons to front band opposite buttonholes.

Finished Bust/Chest Circumference

36	38	40	42	44	46	48	50	52	54"
91.5	96.5	101.5	106.5	112	117	122	127	132	137 cm

Pullover Back

CO:

GAUGE										
3	54	56	60	62	66	70	72	76	78	82 sts.
4	72	76	80	84	88	92	96	100	104	108
5	90	94	100	106	110	116	120	126	130	136
6	108	114	120	126	132	138	144	150	156	162
7	126	134	140	148	154	162	168	176	182	190

Work edging of choice (see page 70), then cont even until piece measures desired length from beg, or about:

13	13	13½	14	14	14½	15	15	15½	16"
33	33	34.5	35.5	35.5	37	38	38	39.5	40.5 cm

Shape armholes

At beg of next 2 rows BO:

3	3	3	3	3	3	4	4	5	5	6 sts.
4	4	4	4	4	4	4	5	5	5	6
5	5	5	5	5	5	5	6	6	6	7
6	6	6	6	6	6	6	7	7	7	8
7	7	7	7	7	7	7	8	9	9	10

At beg of foll 2 rows BO:

3	2	2	2	2	2	2	2	2	2	2 sts.
4	3	3	3	3	3	3	3	3	3	3
5	3	3	3	3	3	3	3	3	3	3
6	4	4	4	4	4	4	4	4	4	4
7	4	4	4	4	4	4	4	4	4	4

Dec 1 st each end of needle every RS row:

3	2	2	3	3	4	4	4	4	4	4 times.
4	3	3	4	5	5	5	5	6	7	7
5	3	4	5	5	5	6	6	8	9	9
6	4	5	6	6	6	7	8	9	11	11
7	5	5	6	7	7	9	9	10	12	12

There will remain:

3	40	42	44	46	48	50	52	54	56	58 sts.
4	52	56	58	60	64	68	70	72	74	76
5	68	70	74	80	84	88	90	92	94	98
6	80	84	88	94	100	104	106	110	112	116
7	94	102	106	112	118	122	126	130	132	138

Cont even until armholes measure:

9	9½	9½	9¾	10	11	11½	12	12½	13"
23	24	24	25	25.5	28	29	30.5	31.5	33 cm

Shape shoulders

At beg of next 2 rows BO:

3	5	5	6	5	5	5	5	5	5	5 sts.
4	7	8	6	6	6	7	7	7	7	7
5	6	7	7	8	8	9	9	9	9	9
6	7	8	8	9	10	10	10	11	10	11
7	8	10	10	11	11	11	12	12	12	13

At beg of foll 2 rows BO:

3	5	6	6	5	5	5	5	5	5	5 sts.
4	6	7	5	5	6	6	6	7	7	7
5	6	6	7	8	8	8	8	8	9	9
6	7	7	8	9	10	10	10	10	10	11
7	8	9	10	11	11	11	12	12	12	13

At beg of foll 2 rows BO (if number is zero, omit these rows):

3	0	0	0	3	4	4	4	5	5	6 sts.
4	0	0	5	5	6	6	6	6	6	7
5	6	6	7	7	8	8	8	8	8	9
6	7	7	8	9	9	10	9	10	10	10
7	8	9	10	10	12	12	11	12	12	12

BO rem sts for back neck:

3	20	20	20	20	20	22	24	24	26	26 sts.
4	26	26	26	28	28	30	32	32	34	34
5	32	32	32	34	36	38	40	42	42	44
6	38	40	40	40	42	44	48	48	52	52
7	46	46	46	48	50	54	56	58	60	62

Pullover Front

Work as for back until armholes measure:

3	3	3	3	3¼	4½	4½	4¾	5	5"
7.5	7.5	7.5	7.5	8.5	11.5	11.5	12	12.5	12.5 cm

Shape V-neck

With RS facing, work to center of row. Turn, and work these sts only to shoulder (place rem sts on a holder to work later). Cont to work armhole shaping as for back, if necessary, and *at the same time,* dec 1 st at neck edge every RS row:

3	10	10	10	10	10	11	12	12	13	13 times.
4	12	12	12	13	13	15	16	16	17	17
5	13	12	12	13	15	16	16	18	18	19
6	16	16	16	16	17	18	21	21	23	23
7	20	20	20	21	22	25	25	27	29	28

Then dec 1 st at neck edge every 4 rows (if number is zero, omit these rows):

3	0	0	0	0	0	0	0	0	0	0 time(s).
4	1	1	1	1	1	0	0	0	0	0
5	3	4	4	4	3	3	4	3	3	3
6	3	4	4	4	4	4	3	3	3	3
7	3	3	3	3	3	2	3	2	1	3

There will remain:

3	10	11	12	13	14	14	14	15	15	16 sts.
4	13	15	16	16	18	19	19	20	20	21
5	18	19	21	23	24	25	25	25	26	27
6	21	22	24	27	29	30	29	31	30	32
7	24	28	30	32	34	34	35	36	36	38

Work even until armhole measures same as back to shoulder. Shape shoulder as for back. Rejoin yarn at neck edge of held sts and work as for first half, reversing neck and shoulder shaping.

Finishing

Block pieces to measurements. With yarn threaded on a tapestry needle, sew one shoulder seam.
Neckband: With RS facing and beg at other shoulder, pick up and knit 1 st for each BO st along back neck, pick up and knit about 3 sts for every 4 rows down to center front neck, M1 (see Glossary) at base of V shaping, pick up and knit about 3 sts for every 4 rows along front to shoulder. Adjust sts if necessary to achieve a full multiple of the edging pattern you've chosen. Work in chosen pattern until neckband measures ¾" (2 cm), or desired length, working a double decrease (sl 2 tog kwise, k1, p2sso) at center point of V every other row. BO all sts in patt. Sew rem shoulder seam.
Armbands: With RS facing and beg at underarm, pick up and knit 3 sts for every 4 rows around armhole, adjusting the number of sts if necessary to achieve a full multiple of the edging pattern you've chosen. Work in chosen pattern until armband measures ¾" (2 cm), or desired length. BO all sts in patt. Sew side seams. Weave in loose ends. Block again, if desired.

Cardigan Back
Work as for pullover version.

Cardigan Left Front
CO:

3	27	28	30	32	33	35	36	38	39	41 sts.
4	36	38	40	42	44	46	48	50	52	54
5	45	47	50	53	55	58	60	63	65	68
6	54	57	60	63	66	69	72	75	78	81
7	63	67	70	74	77	81	84	88	91	95

Work edging of choice, then cont even until piece measures same as back to armhole.

Shape armhole
At beg of next RS row BO:

3	3	3	3	3	3	3	3	4	4	5 sts.
4	4	4	4	4	4	4	5	5	5	6
5	5	5	5	5	5	5	6	6	6	7
6	6	6	6	6	6	6	7	7	7	8
7	7	7	7	7	7	7	8	9	9	10

At beg of next RS row BO:

3	2	2	2	2	2	2	2	2	2	2 sts.
4	3	3	3	3	3	3	3	3	3	3
5	3	3	3	3	3	3	3	3	3	3
6	4	4	4	4	4	4	4	4	4	4
7	4	4	4	4	4	4	4	4	4	4

Dec 1 st at armhole edge (beg of every RS row):

3	2	2	3	3	4	5	5	5	5	5 times.
4	3	3	4	5	5	5	5	6	7	7
5	3	4	5	5	5	6	6	8	9	9
6	4	5	6	6	6	7	8	9	11	11
7	5	5	6	7	7	9	9	10	12	12

There will remain:

3	20	21	22	23	24	25	26	27	28	29 sts.
4	26	28	29	30	32	34	35	36	37	38
5	34	35	37	40	42	44	45	46	47	49
6	40	42	44	47	50	52	53	55	56	58
7	47	51	53	56	59	61	63	65	66	69

Cont even until armhole measures:

3	3	3	3	3¼	4½	4½	4¾	5	5"
7.5	7.5	7.5	7.5	8.5	11.5	11.5	12	12.5	12.5 cm

Shape V-neck

Dec 1 st at neck edge (end of every RS row):

3	10	10	10	10	10	11	12	12	13	13 times.
4	12	12	12	13	13	15	16	16	17	17
5	13	12	12	13	15	16	16	18	18	19
6	16	16	16	16	17	18	21	21	23	23
7	20	20	20	21	22	25	25	27	29	28

Then dec 1 st at neck edge (end of RS row) every 4 rows (if number is zero, omit these rows):

3	0	0	0	0	0	0	0	0	0	0 time(s).
4	1	1	1	1	1	0	0	0	0	0
5	3	4	4	4	3	3	4	3	3	3
6	3	4	4	4	4	4	3	3	3	3
7	3	3	3	3	3	2	3	2	1	3

There will remain:

3	10	11	12	13	14	14	14	15	15	16 sts.
4	13	15	16	16	18	19	19	20	20	21
5	18	19	21	23	24	25	25	25	26	27
6	21	22	24	27	29	30	29	31	30	32
7	24	28	30	32	34	34	35	36	36	38

Cont even until armhole measures:

9	9½	9½	9¾	10	11	11½	12	12½	13"
23	24	24	25	25.5	28	29	30.5	31.5	33 cm

Shape shoulder

At beg of next RS row (armhole edge) BO:

3	5	5	6	5	5	5	5	5	5	5 sts.
4	7	8	6	6	6	7	7	7	7	7
5	6	7	7	8	8	9	9	9	9	9
6	7	8	8	9	10	10	10	11	10	11
7	8	10	10	11	11	11	12	12	12	13

vests

At beg of foll RS row BO:

3	5	6	6	4	5	5	5	5	5	5 sts.
4	6	7	5	5	6	6	6	7	7	7
5	6	6	7	8	8	8	8	8	9	9
6	7	7	8	9	10	10	10	10	10	11
7	8	9	10	11	11	11	12	12	12	13

At beg of foll RS row BO (if number is zero, omit these rows):

3	0	0	0	4	4	4	4	5	5	6 sts.
4	0	0	5	5	6	6	6	6	6	7
5	6	6	7	7	8	8	8	8	8	9
6	7	7	8	9	9	10	9	10	10	10
7	8	9	10	10	12	12	11	12	12	12

Cardigan Right Front

Work as for left front, but reverse shaping (i.e., BO for armhole and shoulder at beg of WS rows; shape neck at beg of RS rows).

Finishing

Block pieces to measurements. With yarn threaded on a tapestry needle, sew shoulder seams. On left front (for females) or right front (for males), mark placement of 5 or 6 buttons, one ½" (1.3 cm) up from CO edge, one at beg of neck shaping, and the others evenly spaced in between.

Neck/front band: With RS facing and beg at lower right front edge, pick up and knit about 3 sts for every 4 rows along front to shoulder, pick up and knit 1 st for each BO st along back neck, pick up and knit about 3 sts for every 4 rows down left front. Adjust sts if necessary to achieve a full multiple of the edging pattern you've chosen. Work in chosen pattern until band measures ¾" (2 cm), working one-row buttonholes (see Glossary) opposite markers (on right front for females; left front for males) when band measures between ¼" and ½" (.6 cm and 1.3 cm). BO all sts in patt. Sew buttons to front band opposite buttonholes.

Armbands: With RS facing and beg at underarm, pick up and knit 3 sts for every 4 rows around armhole, adjusting the number of sts if necessary to achieve a full multiple of the edging pattern you've chosen. Work in chosen pattern until band measures ¾" (2 cm), or desired length. BO all sts in patt. Sew side seams. Weave in loose ends.

vests

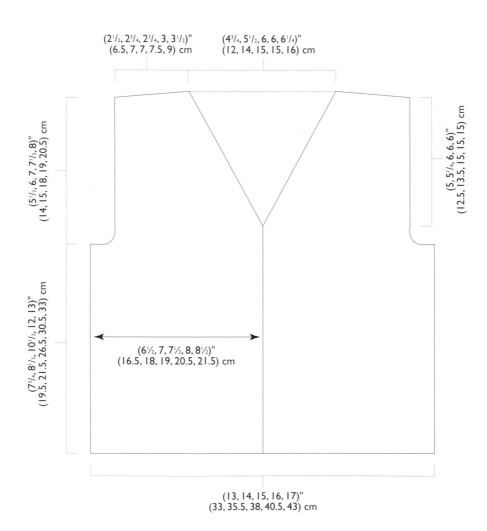

(2½, 2¾, 2¾, 3, 3½)"
(6.5, 7, 7, 7.5, 9) cm

(4¾, 5½, 6, 6, 6¼)"
(12, 14, 15, 15, 16) cm

(5½, 6, 7, 7½, 8)"
(14, 15, 18, 19, 20.5) cm

(5, 5¼, 6, 6, 6)"
(12.5, 13.5, 15, 15, 15) cm

(7¾, 8½, 10½, 12, 13)"
(19.5, 21.5, 26.5, 30.5, 33) cm

(6½, 7, 7½, 8, 8½)"
(16.5, 18, 19, 20.5, 21.5) cm

(13, 14, 15, 16, 17)"
(33, 35.5, 38, 40.5, 43) cm

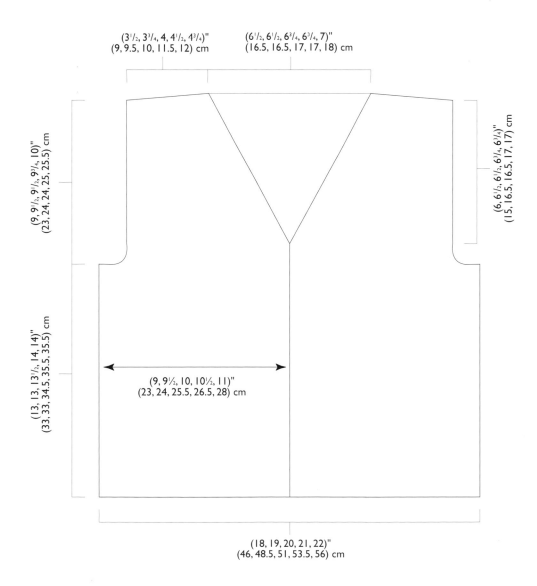

(3½, 3¾, 4, 4½, 4¾)"
(9, 9.5, 10, 11.5, 12) cm

(6½, 6½, 6¾, 6¾, 7)"
(16.5, 16.5, 17, 17, 18) cm

(9, 9½, 9½, 9¾, 10)"
(23, 24, 24, 25, 25.5) cm

(6, 6½, 6½, 6¾, 6¾)"
(15, 16.5, 16.5, 17, 17) cm

(13, 13, 13½, 14, 14)"
(33, 33, 34.5, 35.5, 35.5) cm

(9, 9½, 10, 10½, 11)"
(23, 24, 25.5, 26.5, 28) cm

(18, 19, 20, 21, 22)"
(46, 48.5, 51, 53.5, 56) cm

vests

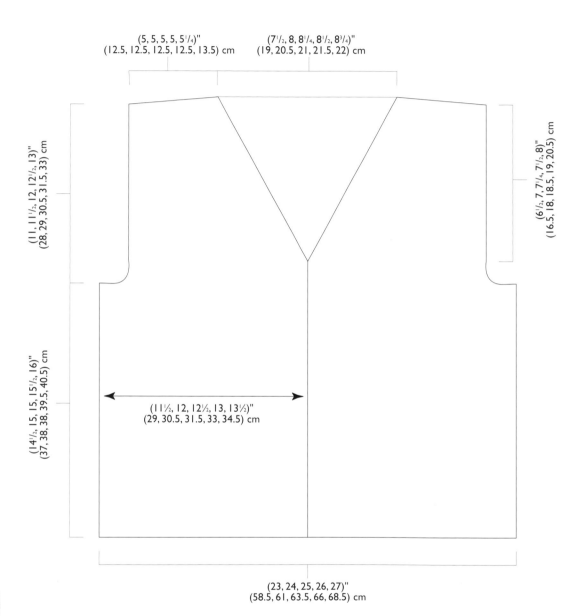

(5, 5, 5, 5, 5¼)"
(12.5, 12.5, 12.5, 12.5, 13.5) cm

(7½, 8, 8¼, 8½, 8¾)"
(19, 20.5, 21, 21.5, 22) cm

(11, 11½, 12, 12½, 13)"
(28, 29, 30.5, 31.5, 33) cm

(6½, 7, 7¼, 7½, 8)"
(16.5, 18, 18.5, 19, 20.5) cm

(14½, 15, 15, 15½, 16)"
(37, 38, 38, 39.5, 40.5) cm

(11½, 12, 12½, 13, 13½)"
(29, 30.5, 31.5, 33, 34.5) cm

(23, 24, 25, 26, 27)"
(58.5, 61, 63.5, 66, 68.5) cm

quick**tips**

- For a loose, drapey look, work the yarn at a looser gauge than recommended.

- Alter the length as you wish—from a belly-baring midriff to an ankle-length tunic—by adjusting the number of rows you knit before starting the armhole shaping. Remember that altering the length will affect the amount of yarn you'll need.

- Work all garment pieces on circular needles. The weight of the knitting will rest comfortably in your lap, and there'll be no chance of poking the arms of your chair (or neighbor) with the needles.

- If you are unsure about what type of lower edging you want, use a provisional method of casting on (see Glossary), then come back later and work the edging downward from the cast-on row.

- For a snug lower edge, cast on ten- to twenty-percent fewer stitches and work a ribbed edging for the desired length, increasing to the designated number of stitches on the last row of ribbing.

- To make sure that the front and back are the same length and that the seams between them will match perfectly, count the number of rows between the lower edging and first armhole bind-off and make sure the numbers are the same for both pieces.

- When picking up stitches for arm, neck, or front edgings, pick up and knit one stitch for each bound-off stitch along horizontal edges, and about two stitches for every three rows, or three stitches for every four rows along vertical or slanted edges. After working a few rows of the edging, evaluate how it looks—if the edging flares and ripples, you have too many stitches; if the body puckers and bubbles, you have too few stitches.

- For a professional-looking finish, block the individual pieces of the vest before sewing together.

- If you use a novelty or mohair yarn, sew the seams with a smooth yarn of similar weight and color.

- Cardigans knitted at a large gauge of 3 stitches/inch may not need buttonholes— most buttons will fit through the individual stitches without damaging them.

vests

VEST AND SWEATER EDGINGS

To prevent curling, hide uneven edge stitches, and conceal stair-step edges along shaped armholes and necklines, most garments are worked with some type of edging stitch. Depending on the type of edging that's used, a vest or sweater can take on a casual or elegant look. Here are some of the most common edging stitches/techniques.

Garter Stitch

Worked by knitting every stitch in every row, garter stitch forms horizontal bands of "bumps" that are identical on the right and wrong sides of the work. Garter stitch can be worked on any number of stitches.

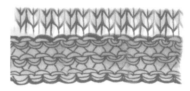

Garter Stitch

Ribbing

Because it alternates columns of knit and purl stitches, ribbing tends to pull in and narrow the width of the knitting. There are a variety of ribbings to use, the most common of which are single rib (alternating one knit stitch with one purl stitch) and double rib (alternating two knit stitches with two purl stitches and shown at right). Single rib is worked on a multiple of two stitches, double rib on a multiple of four. A simple, less elastic, alternative to double rib is mistake rib, in which the columns of knit and purl stitches are offset on alternate rows (see page 44). Mistake rib is worked on a multiple of four stitches, plus three extra stitches to balance the pattern.

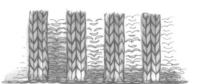

Double Ribbing

I-Cord

I-cord makes a tidy, rounded edge that is sophisticated in its simplicity. It is worked on two double-pointed needles in such a way that a tube is formed (see Glossary). As an edging, it can be worked separately and sewn in place, or attached directly to the edge of the piece as it is knitted. Although I-cord is generally worked on three stitches, you can work it on four, five, or even six stitches for a larger diameter tube.

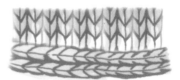

I-Cord

vests

Rolled Edge

A rolled edge appears to be a cross between a garter edge and an I-cord edge. A rolled edge can be worked on any number of stitches. Simply work stockinette stitch for desired length of roll. To control the amount of roll, work a few rows of single or double rib (adjusting the stitch number if necessary to accommodate the pattern repeat) between the roll and the vest or sweater body.

Rolled Edge

Hemmed Edge

A hem gives a clean, straight line without any interruption to the vest or sweater body. Begin with needles a size smaller than you use to get gauge. Work stockinette stitch for the length of the facing, then work a turning row (purl one right-side row, or knit one wrong-side row). Change to the larger needles and work stockinette stitch for the same length as the facing. Join the facing to the body on the next (right-side) row as follows: Fold the facing to the inside and knit each stitch on the needle together with the edge loop of the corresponding stitch of the cast-on row. A hemmed edge can be worked on any number of stitches. For a delicate variation, work a picot turning row as follows: *Knit two stitches together, yarnover; repeat from *.

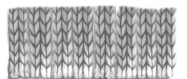

Hemmed Edge

vests

sweaters

basic anatomy

Like the vests on page 57, these sweaters are worked in pieces—back, front(s), and sleeves—from the lower edges upward. Decreases are used to shape the armholes and front neck; increases are used to widen the sleeves at the upper arm. For the pullover version, the front is identical to the back to about two inches short of the shoulder, at which point stitches are decreased to shape the neck. For the cardigan version, the front is worked in two pieces—each with half the number of stitches used for the back. After the pieces are blocked, they are sewn together and the neck is finished off with the desired edging.

This sweater pattern features a loose lower edge, crew neck, and a hip length. For a V-neck, simply follow the instructions for the front neck shaping of the vest. For edging options, see pages 70–71.

To make a sweater following this chart, you need to choose yarn, determine your gauge (see page 6), and pick a size and match it to the finished bust/chest circumference. Gauge runs vertically along the left side of the chart; finished bust/chest circumference is listed horizontally across the top. The child chart begins on page 74; the adult chart begins on page 80. Schematics for all sizes begin on page 90.

All sweaters shown in yarn from Classic Elite Yarns: Gatsby (#2132 raspberry) at 3 stitches/inch; Montera (#3881 lime green) at 4 stitches/inch; Waterspun (#5072 light teal) at 5 stitches/inch.

To Fit Sizes

2 (4, 6, 8, 10) years.

Finished Chest Circumference

26 (28 30 32 34)"
66 (71 76 81.5 86.5) cm

Finished Chest Circumference

26	28	30	32	34"
66	71	76	81.5	86.5 cm

what you'll need

- **Yarn** About 1,000–1,400 yards (925–1,275 m) for child sizes; about 1,400–3,000 yards (1,275–2,750 m) for adult sizes. Exact amount will depend on sweater size and yarn gauge.

- **Needles** Straight needles in size necessary to obtain the desired gauge, and one size smaller for finishing.

- **Notions** Tapestry needle; buttons for cardigan: 7 for child, 8 or 9 for adult.

Pullover Back

CO:

GAUGE					
3	40	42	46	48	52 sts.
4	52	56	60	64	68
5	64	70	74	80	86
6	78	84	90	96	102
7	90	98	106	112	120

Work edging of choice (see pages 70 and 71), then cont even until piece measures desired length from beg, or about:

7¾	8½	10½	12	13"
19.5	21.5	26.5	30.5	33 cm

Shape armholes

At beg of next 2 rows, BO:

3	2	2	2	2	3 sts.
4	3	3	3	3	3
5	4	4	4	4	4
6	5	5	5	5	5
7	5	5	5	5	6

At beg of foll 2 rows, BO:

3	2	2	2	2	2 sts.
4	3	3	3	3	3
5	3	3	3	3	3
6	4	4	4	4	4
7	4	4	4	4	4

Dec I st each end of needle every RS row:

3	1	1	1	2	2 time(s).
4	1	1	1	2	2
5	1	1	1	3	2
6	1	1	1	2	2
7	2	2	2	3	3

There will remain:

3	30	32	36	36	38 sts.
4	38	42	46	48	52
5	48	54	58	60	68
6	58	64	70	74	80
7	68	76	84	88	94

Cont even until armholes measure:

5½	6¾	7¼	7½	8"
14	17	18.5	19	20.5 cm

Shape shoulders

At beg of next 2 rows (each armhole edge) BO:

3	4	4	4	4	5 sts.
4	5	5	6	6	7
5	6	7	7	8	6
6	7	6	6	7	8
7	6	7	7	8	9

At beg of foll 2 rows BO:

3	4	4	5	5	5 sts.
4	4	5	5	6	7
5	6	7	7	7	6
6	7	5	6	6	7
7	5	6	7	8	8

At beg of foll 2 rows BO (if number is zero, omit these 2 rows):

3	0	0	0	0	0 sts.
4	0	0	0	0	0
5	0	0	0	0	6
6	0	5	5	6	7
7	5	6	6	7	8

BO rem sts for back neck:

3	14	16	18	18	18 sts.
4	20	22	24	24	24
5	24	26	30	30	32
6	30	32	36	36	36
7	36	38	44	42	44

Pullover Front

Work as for back until armholes measure:

4	5¼	5¾	6	6½"
10	13.5	14.5	15	16.5 cm

There will be:

3	30	32	36	36	38 sts.
4	38	42	46	48	52
5	48	54	58	60	68
6	58	64	70	74	80
7	68	76	84	88	94

Shape crewneck

With RS facing, work across:

3	12	12	13	13	14 sts,
4	15	16	16	17	19
5	19	20	21	22	26
6	23	24	25	27	30
7	27	28	30	32	35

join new yarn and BO for front neck:

3	6	8	10	10	10 sts,
4	8	10	14	14	14
5	10	14	16	16	16
6	12	16	20	20	20
7	14	20	24	24	24

work to end. There will be the following number of sts at each side:

3	12	12	13	13	14 sts.
4	15	16	16	17	19
5	19	20	21	22	26
6	23	24	25	27	30
7	27	28	30	32	35

Working each side separately, at each neck edge BO 3 sts (if number is zero, omit these rows):

3	0	0	0	0	0 time(s).
4	0	0	0	0	0
5	1	0	1	1	1
6	1	1	1	1	1
7	2	1	1	1	1

Then BO 2 sts:

3	1	1	1	1	1 time(s).
4	2	2	1	1	1
5	1	2	1	1	1
6	2	1	1	1	1
7	1	2	2	2	2

Then dec 1 st every RS row:

3	2	2	2	2	2 times.
4	2	2	3	3	3
5	2	2	2	2	3
6	2	3	3	3	3
7	3	2	3	2	3

There will remain the following number of sts at each side:

3	8	8	9	9	10 sts.
4	9	10	11	12	14
5	12	14	14	15	18
6	14	16	17	19	22
7	16	19	20	23	25

Work even until armhole measures same as back to shoulder. Shape shoulders as for back, working bind-offs at each armhole edge.

Sleeves

CO:

3	18	20	22	22	24 sts.
4	24	26	28	30	32
5	30	32	36	38	40
6	36	40	42	46	48
7	42	46	48	52	56

Work edging of choice until piece measures:

1½	1½	1½	2	2"
3.8	3.8	3.8	5	5 cm

Change to St st and inc 1 st each end of needle every 6 rows (if number is zero, omit these rows):

3	6	6	8	8	8 time(s).
4	3	3	7	8	9
5	0	3	5	6	8
6	1	0	4	6	6
7	5	4	7	9	12

Then inc 1 st each end of needle every 4 rows:

3	2	3	1	2	3 time(s).
4	8	10	6	5	5
5	14	14	11	10	10
6	16	19	16	13	15
7	14	18	16	14	13

There will remain:

3	34	38	40	42	46 sts.
4	46	52	54	56	60
5	58	66	68	70	76
6	70	78	82	84	90
7	80	90	94	98	106

Work even until piece measures:

12	13	14	15	16"
30.5	33	35.5	38	40.5 cm

or desired length to armhole.

Shape cap

At beg of next 2 rows, BO:

3	2	2	2	2	3 sts.
4	3	3	3	3	3
5	4	4	4	4	4
6	5	5	5	5	5
7	5	5	5	5	6

At beg of foll 2 rows, BO:

3	2	2	2	2	2 sts.
4	3	3	3	3	3
5	3	3	3	3	3
6	4	4	4	4	4
7	4	4	4	4	4

Dec 1 st each end of needle every RS row:

3	1	1	1	2	2 time(s).
4	1	1	1	2	2
5	1	1	1	2	2
6	1	1	1	2	2
7	2	2	2	3	3

There will remain:

3	24	28	30	30	32 sts.
4	32	38	40	40	44
5	42	50	52	52	58
6	50	58	62	62	68
7	58	68	72	74	80

Dec 1 st each end of needle every 4 rows (if number is zero, omit these rows):

3	0	0	1	1	1 time(s).
4	0	0	1	0	1
5	0	0	0	0	0
6	0	0	2	1	1
7	0	0	2	2	3

Dec 1 st each end of needle every RS row (if number is zero, omit these rows):

3	0	1	1	1	2 time(s).
4	1	3	3	5	3
5	2	3	7	5	8
6	2	2	3	6	4
7	2	5	4	5	4

BO 2 sts at beg of next (if number is zero, omit these rows):

3	2	2	2	2	2 rows.
4	0	2	2	2	4
5	4	4	2	4	4
6	0	4	2	2	4
7	4	2	4	4	4

BO 3 sts at beg of next:

3	4	4	4	4	4 rows.
4	4	2	2	2	2
5	6	6	6	6	6
6	6	8	6	6	10
7	2	2	2	2	4

BO 4 sts at beg of next (if number is zero, omit these rows):

3	0	0	0	0	0 rows.
4	2	2	2	2	2
5	0	0	0	0	0
6	4	2	4	4	2
7	6	6	6	6	6

BO rem:

3	8	10	10	10	10 sts.
4	10	14	14	12	14
5	12	18	16	16	16
6	12	14	14	10	12
7	16	24	22	22	22

Finishing

Block pieces to measurements. With yarn threaded on a tapestry needle, sew one shoulder seam.

Neckband: With smaller needles, RS facing, and beg at other shoulder, pick up and knit 1 st for each BO st along back neck, pick up and knit about 3 sts for every 4 rows down to center front neck, pick up and knit 1 st for each BO st along front neck, pick up and knit about 3 sts for every 4 rows up to shoulder. Adjust sts if necessary to achieve a full multiple of the edging pattern you've chosen. Work in chosen pattern until neckband measures ¾" (2 cm), or desired length. BO all sts in patt. *Seams:* Sew rem shoulder seam. Sew sleeves into armholes. Sew sleeve and side seams. Weave in loose ends. Block again, if desired.

Cardigan Back

Work as for pullover version.

Cardigan Left Front
CO:

3	20	21	23	24	26 sts.
4	26	28	30	32	34
5	32	35	37	40	43
6	39	42	45	48	51
7	45	49	53	56	60

Work edging of choice (as for back), then cont even until piece measures same as back to armhole.

Shape armhole
At beg of next RS row, BO:

3	2	2	2	2	3 sts.
4	3	3	3	3	3
5	4	4	4	4	4
6	5	5	5	5	5
7	5	5	5	5	6

At beg of next RS row, BO:

3	2	2	2	2	2 sts.
4	3	3	3	3	3
5	3	3	3	3	3
6	4	4	4	4	4
7	4	4	4	4	4

Dec 1 st at arm edge every RS row:

3	1	1	1	2	2 time(s).
4	1	1	1	2	2
5	1	1	1	3	2
6	1	1	1	2	2
7	2	2	2	3	3

There will remain:

3	15	16	18	18	19 sts.
4	19	21	23	24	26
5	24	27	29	30	34
6	29	32	35	37	40
7	34	38	42	44	47

Cont even until armhole measures

	4	5¼	5¾	6	6½"
	10	13.5	14.5	15	16.5 cm

ending with a RS row.

Shape crewneck
With WS facing, BO

3	3	4	5	5	5 sts,
4	4	5	7	7	7
5	5	7	8	8	8
6	6	8	10	10	10
7	7	10	12	12	12

work to end.

At neck edge, BO 3 sts (if number is zero, omit these rows):

3	0	0	0	0	0 time(s).
4	0	0	0	0	0
5	1	0	1	1	1
6	1	1	1	1	1
7	2	1	1	1	1

Then BO 2 sts:

3	1	1	1	1	1 time(s).
4	2	2	1	1	1
5	1	2	1	1	1
6	2	1	1	1	1
7	1	2	2	2	2

Then dec 1 st at neck edge every RS row:

3	2	2	2	2	2 times.
4	2	2	3	3	3
5	2	2	2	2	3
6	2	3	3	3	3
7	3	2	3	2	3

There will remain:

3	8	8	9	9	10 sts.
4	9	10	11	12	14
5	12	14	14	15	18
6	14	16	17	19	22
7	16	19	20	23	25

Cont even until armhole measures:

5½	6¾	7¼	7½	8"
14	17	18.5	19	20.5 cm

Shape shoulder

At beg of next RS row BO:

3	4	4	4	4	5 sts.
4	5	5	6	6	7
5	6	7	7	8	6
6	7	6	6	7	8
7	6	7	7	8	9

At beg of foll RS row BO:

3	4	4	5	5	5 sts.
4	4	5	5	6	7
5	6	7	7	7	6
6	7	5	6	6	7
7	5	6	7	8	8

At beg of foll RS row BO (if number is zero, omit these rows):

3	0	0	0	0	0 sts.
4	0	0	0	0	0
5	0	0	0	0	6
6	0	5	5	6	7
7	5	6	6	7	8

Cardigan Right Front

Work as for left front, but reverse shaping (i.e., BO for armhole and shoulder at beg of WS rows; shape neck at beg of RS rows).

Cardigan Sleeves

Work as for pullover version.

Finishing

Block pieces to measurements. With yarn threaded on a tapestry needle, sew shoulder seams. On left front (for females) or right front (for males), mark placement of 5 buttons, one ½" (1.3 cm) up from CO edge, one at beg of neck shaping, and the others evenly spaced in between. *Neckband:* With smaller needles, pick up and knit 3 sts for every 4 rows and 1 st for every BO st around neck opening. Adjust sts if necessary to achieve a full multiple of the edging pattern you've chosen. Work edging pattern of choice for ¾" (2 cm). *Button band:* (on left front for females; right front for males) With RS facing, pick up and knit about 3 sts for every 4 rows along center front edge. Adjust sts if necessary to achieve a full multiple of the edging pattern you've chosen. Work in chosen pattern until band measures ¾" (2 cm). *Buttonhole band:* (on right front for females; left front for males) Work as for button band, working one-row buttonholes (see Glossary) opposite markers when band measures between ¼" and ½" (.6 and 1.3 cm). BO all sts in patt. *Seams:* Sew sleeves into armholes. Sew sleeve and side seams. Weave in loose ends. Sew buttons to button band opposite buttonholes. Block again, if desired.

Finished Bust/Chest Circumference

36	38	40	42	44	46	48	50	52	54"
91.5	96.5	101.5	106.5	112	117	122	127	132	137 cm

Pullover Back

CO:

GAUGE										
3	54	58	60	64	66	70	72	76	78	82 sts.
4	72	76	80	84	88	92	96	100	104	108
5	90	94	100	106	110	116	120	126	130	136
6	108	114	120	126	132	138	144	150	156	162
7	126	134	140	148	154	162	168	176	182	190

Work edging of choice (see pages 70 and 71), then cont even until piece measures desired length from beg, or about:

13½	14	14½	15	15	15½	16	16	16½	17"
34.5	35.5	37	38	38	39.5	40.5	40.5	42	43 cm

Shape armholes

At beg of next 2 rows, BO:

3	3	3	3	3	3	3	3	4	4	5 sts.
4	4	4	4	4	4	4	5	5	5	6
5	5	5	5	5	5	5	6	6	6	7
6	6	6	6	6	6	6	7	7	7	8
7	7	7	7	7	7	7	8	9	9	10

At beg of foll 2 rows, BO:

3	2	2	2	2	2	2	2	2	2	2 sts.
4	3	3	3	3	3	3	3	3	3	3
5	3	3	3	3	3	3	3	3	3	3
6	4	4	4	4	4	4	4	4	4	4
7	4	4	4	4	4	4	4	4	4	4

Dec 1 st each end of needle every RS row:

3	2	3	3	3	4	4	4	5	5	5 times.
4	3	3	4	4	4	5	5	6	7	7
5	3	4	5	5	5	6	6	8	9	9
6	4	5	6	6	6	7	8	9	11	11
7	5	5	7	7	7	9	9	10	12	12

There will remain:

3	40	42	44	48	48	52	54	54	56	58 sts.
4	52	56	58	62	66	68	70	72	74	76
5	68	70	74	80	84	88	90	92	94	98
6	80	84	88	94	100	104	106	110	112	116
7	94	102	104	112	118	122	126	130	132	138

Cont even until armholes measure:

9	9½	9½	9¾	10	11	11½	12	12½	13"
23	24	24	25	25.5	28	29	30.5	31.5	33 cm

Shape shoulders

At beg of next 2 rows (each armhole edge) BO:

3	5	5	6	5	5	5	5	5	5	5 sts.
4	7	8	6	6	6	7	7	7	7	7
5	6	7	7	8	8	9	9	9	9	9
6	7	8	8	9	10	10	10	11	10	11
7	8	10	10	11	11	11	12	12	12	13

At beg of foll 2 rows BO:

3	5	6	6	5	5	5	5	5	5	5 sts.
4	6	7	5	6	6	6	6	7	7	7
5	6	6	7	8	8	8	8	8	9	9
6	7	7	8	9	10	10	10	10	10	11
7	8	9	10	11	11	11	12	12	12	13

At beg of foll 2 rows BO (if number is zero, omit these 2 rows):

3	0	0	0	4	4	5	5	5	5	6 sts.
4	0	0	5	5	7	6	6	6	6	7
5	6	6	7	7	8	8	8	8	8	9
6	7	7	8	9	9	10	9	10	10	10
7	8	9	9	10	12	12	11	12	12	12

BO rem sts for back neck:

3	20	20	20	20	20	22	24	24	26	26 sts.
4	26	26	26	28	28	30	32	32	34	34
5	32	32	32	34	36	38	40	42	42	44
6	38	40	40	40	42	44	48	48	52	52
7	46	46	46	48	50	54	56	58	60	62

Pullover Front

Work as for back until armholes measure:

7	7½	7½	7¾	8	9	9½	10	10½	11"
18	19	19	19.5	20.5	23	24	25.5	26.5	28 cm

There will be:

3	40	42	44	48	48	52	54	54	56	58 sts.
4	52	56	58	62	66	68	70	72	74	76
5	68	70	74	80	84	88	90	92	94	98
6	80	84	88	94	100	104	106	110	112	116
7	94	102	104	112	118	122	126	130	132	138

Shape crewneck

With RS facing, work across:

3	15	16	17	19	18	20	21	21	21	22 sts,
4	19	21	22	24	25	26	27	28	28	29
5	26	27	29	32	32	34	35	36	36	38
6	30	32	34	37	38	40	41	43	43	45
7	35	39	40	44	45	47	49	51	51	54

join new yarn and BO for front neck:

3	10	10	10	10	12	12	12	12	14	14 sts,
4	14	14	14	14	16	16	16	16	18	18
5	16	16	16	16	20	20	20	20	22	22
6	20	20	20	20	24	24	24	24	26	26
7	24	24	24	24	28	28	28	28	30	30

work to end. There will be the following number of sts at each side:

3	15	16	17	19	18	20	21	21	21	22 sts.
4	19	21	22	24	25	26	27	28	28	29
5	26	27	29	32	32	34	35	36	36	38
6	30	32	34	37	38	40	41	43	43	45
7	35	39	40	44	45	47	49	51	51	54

Working each side separately, at each neck edge BO 3 sts (if number is zero, omit these rows):

3	0	0	0	0	0	0	0	0	0	0 time(s).
4	0	0	0	0	0	0	1	1	1	1
5	1	1	1	1	1	1	2	2	2	2
6	1	2	2	2	1	2	2	2	2	2
7	2	2	2	2	2	2	2	2	2	3

Then BO 2 sts:

3	1	1	1	1	1	1	2	2	2	2 time(s).
4	2	2	2	2	2	2	1	1	1	1
5	1	1	1	2	1	2	1	1	1	1
6	2	1	1	1	2	1	2	2	2	2
7	1	1	1	2	1	2	3	3	3	2

Then dec 1 st every RS row:

3	3	3	3	3	2	3	2	2	2	2 times.
4	2	2	2	3	2	3	3	3	3	3
5	3	3	3	2	3	2	2	3	2	3
6	2	2	2	2	2	2	2	2	3	3
7	3	3	3	2	3	3	2	3	3	3

There will remain the following number of sts at each side:

3	10	11	12	14	14	15	15	15	15	16 sts.
4	13	15	16	17	19	19	19	20	20	21
5	18	19	21	23	24	25	25	25	26	27
6	21	22	24	27	29	30	29	31	30	32
7	24	28	29	32	34	34	35	36	36	38

Work even until armhole measures same as back to shoulder. Shape shoulders as for back, working bind-offs at each armhole edge.

Sleeves

CO:

3	28	28	30	30	30	30	32	32	34	34 sts.
4	38	38	40	40	40	44	44	44	46	46
5	46	46	50	50	50	54	54	56	58	58
6	56	56	60	60	60	66	66	66	68	68
7	66	66	70	70	70	76	76	76	80	80

Work edging of choice until piece measures:

2½	2½	2½	2½	2½	2½	2½	2½	2½	2½"
6.5	6.5	6.5	6.5	6.5	6.5	6.5	6.5	6.5	6.5 cm

Change to St st and inc 1 st each end of needle every 6 rows:

3	10	10	10	10	11	8	10	11	11	12 times.
4	10	9	13	13	14	13	14	12	14	13
5	7	9	14	14	11	13	13	13	12	12
6	8	10	12	12	12	14	14	12	10	10
7	14	16	21	19	18	22	20	16	21	19

Then inc 1 st each end of needle every 4 rows (if number is zero, omit these rows):

3	0	0	0	0	0	3	1	1	0	0 time(s).
4	3	4	0	0	0	0	0	3	1	3
5	10	8	2	2	7	4	5	5	7	8
6	12	10	8	8	9	6	7	11	13	15
7	9	7	1	4	7	1	5	11	6	9

There will remain:

3	48	48	50	50	52	52	54	56	56	58 sts.
4	64	64	66	66	68	70	72	74	76	78
5	80	80	82	82	86	88	90	92	96	98
6	96	96	100	100	102	106	108	112	114	118
7	112	112	114	116	120	122	126	130	134	136

Work even until piece measures:

	16½	17	17½	17½	18	18	18½	18½	19	19½"
	42	43	44.5	44.5	46	46	47	47	48.5	49.5 cm

or desired length to armhole.

Shape cap

At beg of next 2 rows, BO:

3	3	3	3	3	3	3	3	4	4	5 sts.
4	4	4	4	4	4	4	5	5	5	6
5	5	5	5	5	5	5	6	6	6	7
6	6	6	6	6	6	6	7	7	7	8
7	7	7	7	7	7	7	8	9	9	10

At beg of foll 2 rows, BO:

3	2	2	2	2	2	2	2	2	2	2 sts.
4	3	3	3	3	3	3	3	3	3	3
5	3	3	3	3	3	3	3	3	3	3
6	4	4	4	4	4	4	4	4	4	4
7	4	4	4	4	4	4	4	4	4	4

Dec 1 st each end of needle every RS row:

3	2	3	3	3	4	4	4	5	5	5 times.
4	3	3	4	4	4	5	5	6	7	7
5	3	4	5	5	5	6	6	8	9	9
6	4	5	6	6	6	7	8	9	11	11
7	5	5	7	7	7	9	9	10	12	12

There will remain:

3	34	32	34	34	34	34	36	34	34	34 sts.
4	44	44	44	44	46	46	46	46	46	46
5	58	56	56	56	60	60	60	58	60	60
6	68	66	68	68	70	72	70	72	70	72
7	80	80	78	80	84	82	84	84	84	84

Dec 1 st each end of needle every 4 rows:

3	2	2	2	2	2	3	4	4	5	5 times.
4	2	3	3	3	4	4	5	5	5	6
5	2	3	2	3	3	5	7	7	7	8
6	4	4	4	4	4	5	6	6	6	7
7	4	6	5	6	6	7	8	9	9	11

Dec 1 st each end of needle every RS row (if number is zero, omit these rows):

3	0	3	3	4	4	3	2	3	1	3 time(s).
4	2	3	2	2	2	3	3	3	3	2
5	6	5	6	5	5	3	2	1	2	1
6	2	4	2	3	3	4	3	5	4	4
7	5	3	2	2	3	4	3	3	3	1

BO 2 sts at beg of next (if number is zero, omit these rows):

3	4	2	0	2	2	2	2	0	2	0 rows.
4	4	2	2	2	2	4	2	2	2	2
5	4	2	2	2	4	4	2	2	2	4
6	2	2	2	2	2	4	4	2	2	2
7	4	4	2	4	2	2	2	2	4	4

BO 3 sts at beg of next (if number is zero, omit these rows):

3	4	2	4	2	2	2	2	2	2	2 rows.
4	2	2	2	2	2	0	0	0	0	0
5	6	6	6	6	6	6	6	6	6	6
6	8	6	8	10	8	6	8	8	8	8
7	2	2	4	2	4	2	2	4	2	2

BO 4 sts at beg of next (if number is zero, omit these rows):

3	0	0	0	0	0	0	0	0	0	0 rows.
4	2	2	2	2	2	2	2	2	2	2
5	0	0	0	0	0	0	0	0	0	0
6	4	4	4	2	4	4	2	2	2	2
7	6	6	6	6	6	6	6	4	4	4

BO rem:

3	10	12	12	12	12	12	14	14	12	12 sts.
4	14	14	16	16	16	16	18	18	18	18
5	16	18	18	18	18	18	20	20	20	16
6	12	12	12	12	12	12	12	14	14	14
7	24	24	24	26	26	26	28	28	30	30

Finishing

Block pieces to measurements. With yarn threaded on a tapestry needle, sew one shoulder seam.
Neckband: With smaller needles, RS facing, and beg at other shoulder, pick up and knit 1 st for each BO st along back neck, pick up and knit about 3 sts for every 4 rows down to center front neck, pick up and knit 1 st for each BO st along front neck, pick up and knit about 3 sts for every 4 rows up to shoulder. Adjust sts if necessary to achieve a full multiple of the edging pattern you've chosen. Work in chosen pattern until neckband measures ¾" (2 cm), or desired length. BO all sts in patt.
Seams: Sew rem shoulder seam. Sew sleeves into armholes. Sew sleeve and side seams. Weave in loose ends. Block again, if desired.

Cardigan Back

Work as for pullover version.

Cardigan Left Front
CO:

3	27	28	30	32	33	35	36	38	39	41 sts.
4	36	38	40	42	44	46	48	50	52	54
5	45	47	50	53	55	58	60	63	65	68
6	54	57	60	63	66	69	72	75	78	81
7	63	67	70	74	77	81	84	88	91	95

Work edging of choice, then cont even until piece measures same as back to armhole.

Shape armhole
At beg of next RS row, BO:

3	3	3	3	3	3	3	3	4	4	5 sts.
4	4	4	4	4	4	4	5	5	5	6
5	5	5	5	5	5	5	6	6	6	7
6	6	6	6	6	6	6	7	7	7	8
7	7	7	7	7	7	7	8	9	9	10

At beg of next RS row, BO:

3	2	2	2	2	2	2	2	2	2	2 sts.
4	3	3	3	3	3	3	3	3	3	3
5	3	3	3	3	3	3	3	3	3	3
6	4	4	4	4	4	4	4	4	4	4
7	4	4	4	4	4	4	4	4	4	4

Dec 1 st at arm edge every RS row:

3	2	3	3	3	4	4	4	5	5	5 times.
4	3	3	4	4	4	5	5	6	7	7
5	3	4	5	5	5	6	6	8	9	9
6	4	5	6	6	6	7	8	9	11	11
7	5	5	7	7	7	9	9	10	12	12

There will remain:

3	20	20	22	24	24	26	27	27	28	29 sts.
4	26	28	29	31	33	34	35	36	37	38
5	34	35	37	40	42	44	45	46	47	49
6	40	42	44	47	50	52	53	55	56	58
7	47	51	52	56	59	61	63	65	66	69

Cont even until armhole measures

	7	7½	7½	7¾	8	9	9½	10	10½	11"
	18	19	19	19.5	20.5	23	24	25.5	26.5	28 cm

ending with a RS row.

Shape crewneck

With WS facing, BO

3	5	5	5	5	6	6	6	6	7	7 sts,
4	7	7	7	7	8	8	8	8	9	9
5	8	8	8	8	10	10	10	10	11	11
6	10	10	10	10	12	12	12	12	13	13
7	12	12	12	12	14	14	14	14	15	15

work to end.

At neck edge, BO 3 sts (if number is zero, omit these rows):

3	0	0	0	0	0	0	0	0	0	0 time(s).
4	0	0	0	0	0	0	1	1	1	1
5	1	1	1	1	1	1	2	2	2	2
6	1	2	2	2	1	2	2	2	2	2
7	2	2	2	2	2	2	2	2	2	3

Then BO 2 sts:

3	1	1	1	1	1	1	2	2	2	2 time(s).
4	2	2	2	2	2	2	1	1	1	1
5	1	1	1	2	1	2	1	1	1	1
6	2	1	1	1	2	1	2	2	2	2
7	1	1	1	2	1	2	3	3	3	2

Then dec 1 st at neck edge every RS row:

3	3	2	3	3	2	3	2	2	2	2 times.
4	2	2	2	3	2	3	3	3	3	3
5	3	3	3	2	3	2	2	3	2	3
6	2	2	2	2	2	2	2	2	3	3
7	3	3	3	2	3	3	2	3	3	3

There will remain:

3	10	11	12	14	14	15	15	15	15	16 sts.
4	13	15	16	17	19	19	19	20	20	21
5	18	19	21	23	24	25	25	25	26	27
6	21	22	24	27	29	30	29	31	30	32
7	24	28	29	32	34	34	35	36	36	38

Cont even until armhole measures:

	9	9½	9½	9¾	10	11	11½	12	12½	13"
	23	24	24	25	25.5	28	29	30.5	31.5	33 cm

Shape shoulder

At beg of next RS row BO:

3	5	5	6	5	5	5	5	5	5	5 sts.
4	7	8	6	6	6	7	7	7	7	7
5	6	7	7	8	8	9	9	9	9	9
6	7	8	8	9	10	10	10	11	10	11
7	8	10	10	11	11	11	12	12	12	13

At beg of foll RS row BO:

3	5	6	6	5	5	5	5	5	5	5 sts.
4	6	7	5	6	6	6	6	7	7	7
5	6	6	7	8	8	8	8	8	9	9
6	7	7	8	9	10	10	10	10	10	11
7	8	9	10	11	11	11	12	12	12	13

At beg of foll RS row BO (if number is zero, omit these rows):

3	0	0	0	4	4	5	5	5	5	6 sts.
4	0	0	5	5	7	6	6	6	6	7
5	6	6	7	7	8	8	8	8	8	9
6	7	7	8	9	9	10	9	10	10	10
7	8	9	9	10	12	12	11	12	12	12

Cardigan Right Front

Work as for left front, but reverse shaping (i.e., BO for armhole and shoulder at beg of WS rows; shape neck at beg of RS rows).

Cardigan Sleeves

Work as for pullover version.

Finishing

Block pieces to measurements. With yarn threaded on a tapestry needle, sew shoulder seams. On left front (for females) or right front (for males), mark placement of 7 to 9 buttons, one ½" (1.3 cm) up from CO edge, one at beg of neck shaping, and the others evenly spaced in between.

Neckband: With smaller needles, pick up and knit 3 sts for every 4 rows and 1 st for every BO st around neck opening. Adjust sts if necessary to achieve a full multiple of the edging pattern you've chosen. Work in chosen pattern until band measures 1" (2.5 cm) or desired length. BO all sts in patt.

Button band: (on left front for females; right front for males) With RS facing, pick up and knit about 3 sts for every 4 rows along center front edge. Adjust sts if necessary to achieve a full multiple of the edging pattern chosen. Work in chosen pattern until band measures ¾" (2 cm). BO all sts in patt.

Buttonhole band: (on right front for females; left front for males) Work as for button band, working one-row buttonholes (see Glossary) opposite markers when band measures between ¼" and ½" (.6 cm and 1.3 cm). BO all sts in patt.

Seams: Sew sleeves into armholes. Sew sleeve and side seams. Weave in loose ends. Sew buttons to button band opposite buttonholes. Block again, if desired.

quick**tips**

Quick Tips for sweaters can be found with vest tips on page 69. For **Personal Touches,** see pages 70 and 71.

sweaters

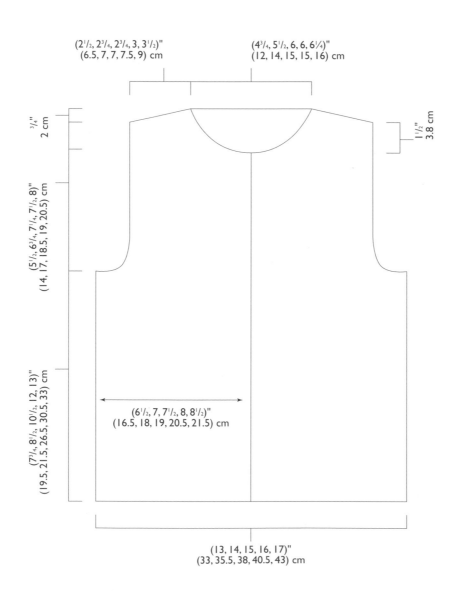

$(2^{1}/_{2}, 2^{3}/_{4}, 2^{3}/_{4}, 3, 3^{1}/_{2})"$
(6.5, 7, 7, 7.5, 9) cm

$(4^{3}/_{4}, 5^{1}/_{2}, 6, 6, 6^{1}/_{4})"$
(12, 14, 15, 15, 16) cm

$^{3}/_{4}"$
2 cm

$1^{1}/_{2}"$
3.8 cm

$(5^{1}/_{2}, 6^{3}/_{4}, 7^{1}/_{4}, 7^{1}/_{2}, 8)"$
(14, 17, 18.5, 19, 20.5) cm

$(7^{3}/_{4}, 8^{1}/_{2}, 10^{1}/_{2}, 12, 13)"$
(19.5, 21.5, 26.5, 30.5, 33) cm

$(6^{1}/_{2}, 7, 7^{1}/_{2}, 8, 8^{1}/_{2})"$
(16.5, 18, 19, 20.5, 21.5) cm

$(13, 14, 15, 16, 17)"$
(33, 35.5, 38, 40.5, 43) cm

child measurements

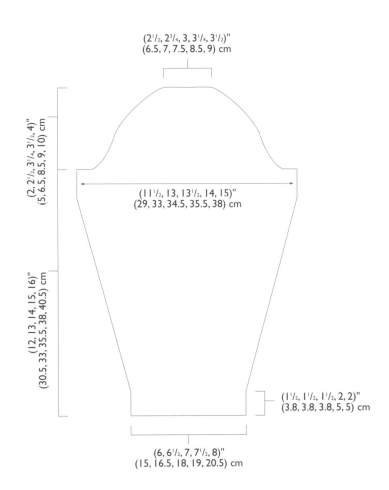

(2¹/₂, 2³/₄, 3, 3¹/₄, 3¹/₂)"
(6.5, 7, 7.5, 8.5, 9) cm

(2, 2¹/₂, 3¹/₄, 3¹/₂, 4)"
(5, 6.5, 8.5, 9, 10) cm

(11¹/₂, 13, 13¹/₂, 14, 15)"
(29, 33, 34.5, 35.5, 38) cm

(12, 13, 14, 15, 16)"
(30.5, 33, 35.5, 38, 40.5) cm

(1¹/₂, 1¹/₂, 1¹/₂, 2, 2)"
(3.8, 3.8, 3.8, 5, 5) cm

(6, 6¹/₂, 7, 7¹/₂, 8)"
(15, 16.5, 18, 19, 20.5) cm

child measurements

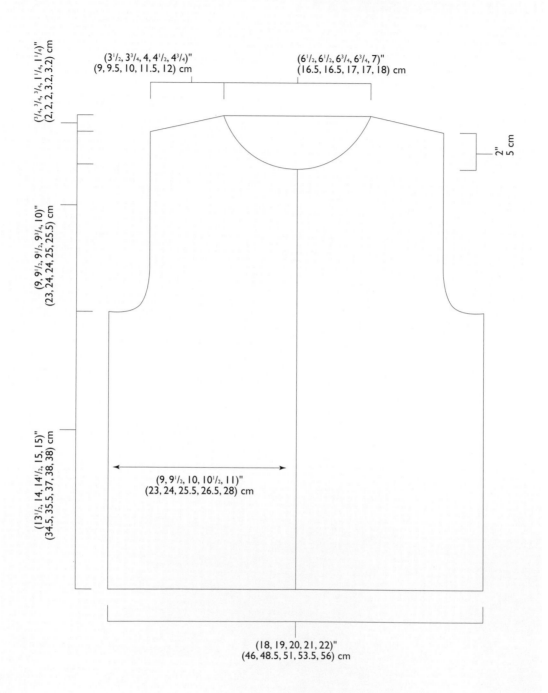

(3¹/₂, 3³/₄, 4, 4¹/₂, 4³/₄)"
(9, 9.5, 10, 11.5, 12) cm

(6¹/₂, 6¹/₂, 6³/₄, 6³/₄, 7)"
(16.5, 16.5, 17, 17, 18) cm

(³/₄, ³/₄, ³/₄, 1¹/₄, 1¹/₄)"
(2, 2, 2, 3.2, 3.2) cm

2"
5 cm

(9, 9¹/₂, 9¹/₂, 9³/₄, 10)"
(23, 24, 24, 25, 25.5) cm

(13¹/₂, 14, 14¹/₂, 15, 15)"
(34.5, 35.5, 37, 38, 38) cm

(9, 9¹/₂, 10, 10¹/₂, 11)"
(23, 24, 25.5, 26.5, 28) cm

(18, 19, 20, 21, 22)"
(46, 48.5, 51, 53.5, 56) cm

36"-44" adult measurements

sweaters

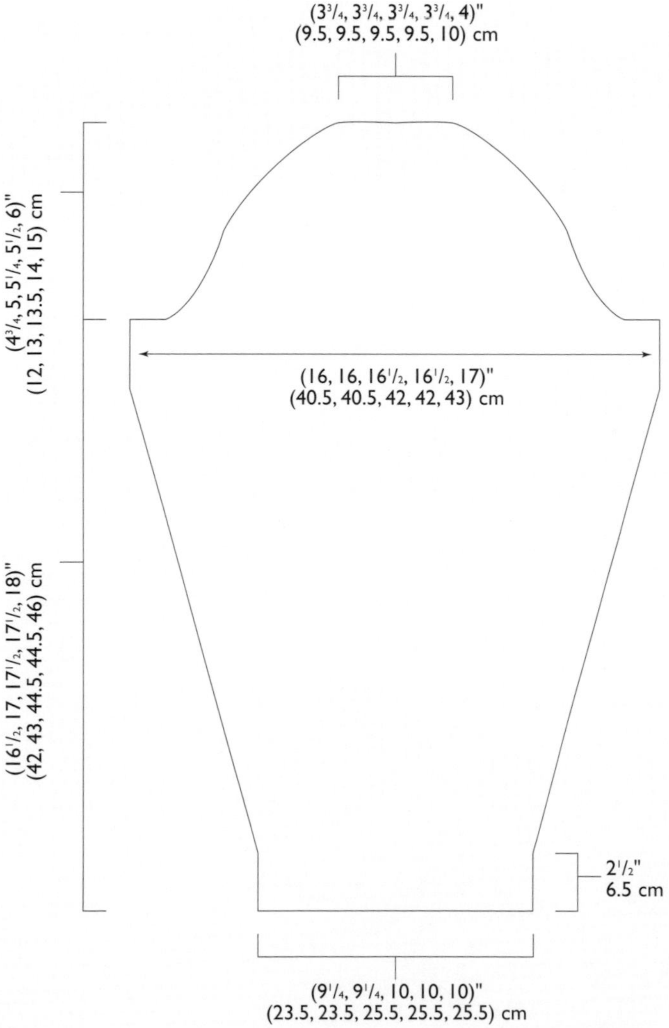

$(3^3/_4, 3^3/_4, 3^3/_4, 3^3/_4, 4)$"
$(9.5, 9.5, 9.5, 9.5, 10)$ cm

$(4^3/_4, 5, 5^1/_4, 5^1/_2, 6)$"
$(12, 13, 13.5, 14, 15)$ cm

$(16, 16, 16^1/_2, 16^1/_2, 17)$"
$(40.5, 40.5, 42, 42, 43)$ cm

$(16^1/_2, 17, 17^1/_2, 17^1/_2, 18)$"
$(42, 43, 44.5, 44.5, 46)$ cm

$2^1/_2$"
6.5 cm

$(9^1/_4, 9^1/_4, 10, 10, 10)$"
$(23.5, 23.5, 25.5, 25.5, 25.5)$ cm

36"-44" adult measurements

sweaters

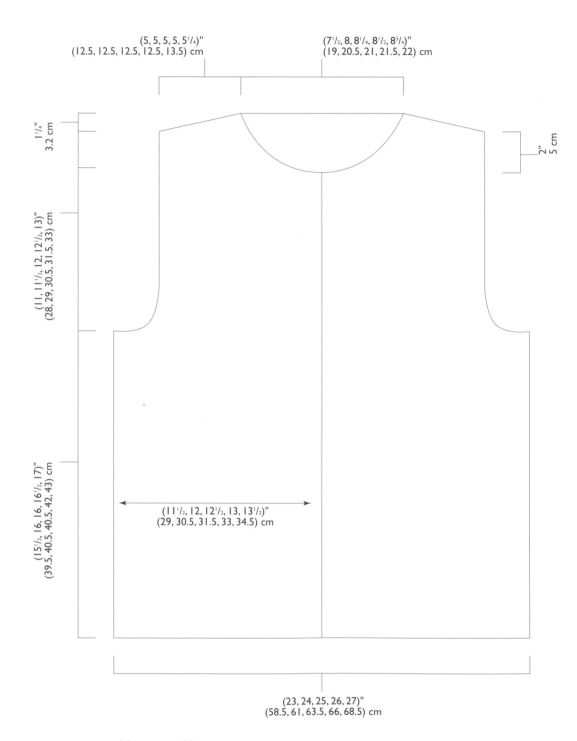

(5, 5, 5, 5, 5¹/₄)"
(12.5, 12.5, 12.5, 12.5, 13.5) cm

(7¹/₂, 8, 8¹/₄, 8¹/₂, 8³/₄)"
(19, 20.5, 21, 21.5, 22) cm

1¹/₄"
3.2 cm

2"
5 cm

(11, 11¹/₂, 12, 12¹/₂, 13)"
(28, 29, 30.5, 31.5, 33) cm

(15¹/₂, 16, 16, 16¹/₂, 17)"
(39.5, 40.5, 40.5, 42, 43) cm

(11¹/₂, 12, 12¹/₂, 13, 13¹/₂)"
(29, 30.5, 31.5, 33, 34.5) cm

(23, 24, 25, 26, 27)"
(58.5, 61, 63.5, 66, 68.5) cm

46"-54" adult measurements

sweaters

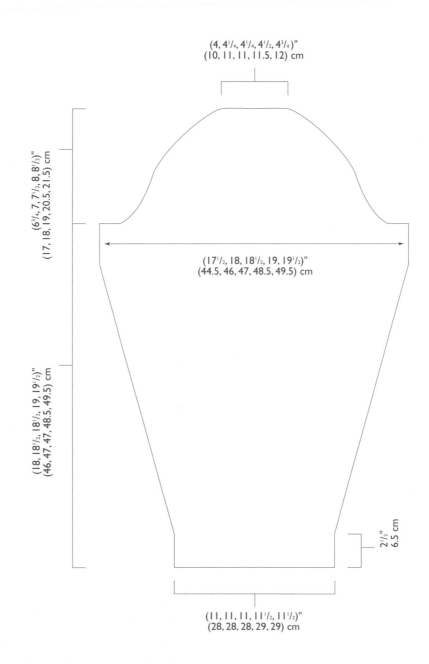

(4, 4¹/₄, 4¹/₄, 4¹/₂, 4³/₄)"
(10, 11, 11, 11.5, 12) cm

(6³/₄, 7, 7¹/₂, 8, 8¹/₂)"
(17, 18, 19, 20.5, 21.5) cm

(17¹/₂, 18, 18¹/₂, 19, 19¹/₂)"
(44.5, 46, 47, 48.5, 49.5) cm

(18, 18¹/₂, 18¹/₂, 19, 19¹/₂)"
(46, 47, 47, 48.5, 49.5) cm

2¹/₂"
6.5 cm

(11, 11, 11, 11¹/₂, 11¹/₂)"
(28, 28, 28, 29, 29) cm

46"-54" adult measurements

Expanding Your Options

If you consider the number of sizes and gauges provided for each of the eight projects in this book, there are more than 350 sets of instructions. Still, that may not be enough. You may want to adjust one of the patterns to accommodate a favorite stitch or color pattern, or you may be in love with a yarn that knits up at a gauge that isn't provided. The following guidelines will help you make these changes with confidence.

Adding Stitch or Color Patterns

The projects in this book are intentionally simple; there is little interruption in the way of shaping. The purpose for this is twofold—first, the patterns are easy to follow; second, each pattern can be looked at as a blank canvas on which to add your own design.

As long as your gauge matches one of the gauges specified for the projects in this book, you can work any of them in any stitch or color pattern you choose—lace, Aran, or Fair Isle, to name a few. Just work out your gauge by knitting a swatch in the pattern you plan to use in the project—chances are that it will be significantly different than one worked in stockinette stitch. But be aware that textured patterns generally take up more yarn than stockinette stitch, and purchase extra yarn accordingly. When planning a stitch or color pattern, take into account the number of stitches in a pattern repeat and the position of the pattern in relation to the overall dimensions of the knitted piece.

If possible, choose a stitch or color pattern that fits into the body of the project an even number of times. Your project will have a more polished and professional look if there are no partial repeats at the ends of rows. For example, if your project has 96 stitches, look for a pattern which repeats over a number of stitches that fits evenly into this number, such as 4, 8, or 12 stitches. To prevent the pattern from being interrupted by a side seam, cast on an extra stitch at each end of the needle and use these extra stitches for the seams. These extra stitches are not necessary for projects worked in the round, which have no seams.

Most stitch or color patterns, except very small ones that repeat over just a few stitches, look best when centered across the knitted piece. Align the focal point of the pattern, such as a cable, with the center stitch on the needles. In general, an odd number of repeats will appear most interesting to the eye—for example, group cables in sets of three, five, or seven.

Be aware that such patterns will be interrupted by the shaping of a knitted piece, such as thumbs on mittens, thumbs and fingers on gloves, heels and toes of socks, decreases on the tops of hats, and the side seams, armholes, necks, and shoulders of sweaters and vests. Ideally, you'll want to plan ahead so that these interruptions fall at convenient points in the pattern repeat, both vertically and horizontally. For example, a mismatched pattern at the shoulder seam on a vest or sweater will be glaringly conspicuous. To make this a "seamless" transition, plan the pattern so that half a repeat falls on the back of the shoulder seam and half falls on the front. Likewise, a glove usually looks more elegant if the color or stitch pattern ends before the fingers are separated. A hat generally looks better if the pattern ends a few rows before the beginning of the top decreases, before the fabric begins to gather and obscure the pattern. The best way to tell that a pattern will be centered both horizontally and vertically is to chart it out, along with the outline of the knitted garment, on graph paper.

Adjusting for a Different Gauge

Sometimes, it will be necessary to adjust the number of stitches you work with in order to center a stitch or color pattern. For example, the vest and sweater instructions in this book are designed to have an even number of stitches across both the front and back. If you choose a stitch or color pattern that has an odd-numbered repeat, you'll be left with an extra stitch on one side. You can leave it as it is, sew the odd stitch in the seam, and be content. Or, you can simply work with one more or one less stitch so that you work with the odd number of stitches that fits your chosen pattern multiple. If you do so, keep the same number of stitches at the shoulders and adjust the number of stitches (plus or minus one stitch) at the neck.

You can further adjust these numbers to accommodate more gauges. All of the instructions in this book are written for gauges of whole numbers of stitches—3, 4, 5, 6, etc. But if you use the schematics provided, it's a simple matter to adjust these instructions for additional gauges, such as fractions.

Let's say you want to knit a vest with a 19" width (38" circumference) at a gauge of 5½ stitches to the inch. The gauge tells us that each inch of knitting will require 5½ stitches. It follows that 19" of knitting will require 19 times that number—19 x 5½ = 104.5 stitches. You'll have to round up to 105 stitches or down to 104 stitches, but in either case, a half stitch will not be noticeable in a total width of 19". If you use the schematics provided to determine the finished width of the upper body, neck, shoulders, etc., and multiply these numbers by the gauge you want, you can calculate the number of stitches to use, then adjust any shaping increases or decreases to correspond.

Another option is to look at the other sizes on the chart. At the gauge of 5 stitches to the inch, the size for a 42" chest requires 105 stitches, which is what you'd need for a 38" chest at 5½ stitches to the inch based on the calculations above. If you follow the stitch requirements for the 42" size and the length measurements for the 38" size, you'll end up with the proper fit without any additional calculations.

Glossary

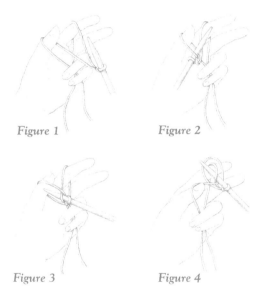

Figure 1

Figure 2

Figure 3

Figure 4

Cast-Ons

Continental (Long-Tail) Cast-On

Leaving a long tail (about ½" to 1" [1.3 to 2.5 cm] for each stitch to be cast on), make a slipknot and place on right needle. Place thumb and index finger between yarn ends so that the working yarn is around your index finger and the tail end is around your thumb. Secure the ends with your other fingers and hold palm upward, making a V of yarn (Figure 1). *Bring needle up through loop on thumb (Figure 2), grab first strand around index finger with needle, and go back down through loop on thumb (Figure 3), drop loop off thumb and, placing thumb back in V configuration, tighten resulting stitch on needle (Figure 4). Repeat from * for desired number of stitches.

Backward Loop Cast-On

*Loop working yarn and place on needle backward so that it doesn't unwind. Repeat from * for desired number of stitches.

Crochet Chain (Provisional) Cast-On

With waste yarn and crochet hook, make a loose crochet chain (see page 104) about four stitches more than you need to cast on. With needle, working yarn, and beginning two stitches from end of chain, pick up and knit one stitch through the back loop of each crochet chain (Figure 1) for desired number of stitches. When you're ready to work in the opposite direction, pull out the crochet chain to expose live stitches (Figure 2).

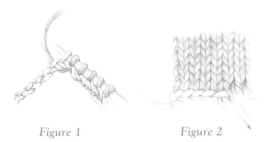

Figure 1   *Figure 2*

Old Norwegian Cast-On

Leaving a long tail (about ½" to 1" [1.3 to 2.5 cm] for each stitch to be cast on), make a slipknot and place on right needle. Place thumb and index finger between yarn ends so that the working yarn is around your index finger and the tail is around your thumb. Secure the ends with your other fingers and hold your palm upward, making a V of yarn (Figure 1). *Bring needle in front of thumb, under both yarns around thumb, down into center of thumb loop, back forward, and over top of yarn around index finger (Figure 2), catch this yarn, and bring needle back down through thumb loop (Figure 3), turning thumb slightly to make room for needle to pass through. Drop loop off thumb (Figure 4) and place thumb back in V configuration while tightening up resulting stitch on needle. Repeat from * for desired number of stitches.

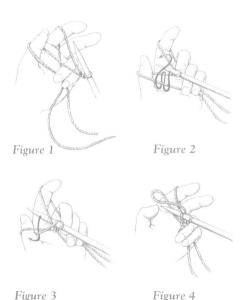

Figure 1   *Figure 2*

Figure 3   *Figure 4*

Figure 1   Figure 2

Invisible (Provisional) Cast-On

Place a loose slipknot on the needle held in your right hand. Hold waste yarn next to slipknot and around your left thumb; hold working yarn over your left index finger. *Bring needle forward under waste yarn, over working yarn, grab a loop of working yarn (Figure 1), then bring needle to the front, over both yarns, and grab a second loop (Figure 2). Repeat from * for desired number of stitches. When you're ready to work in the opposite direction, carefully remove waste yarn to expose live stitches.

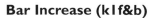

Increases

Raised (M1) Increase

Left Slant

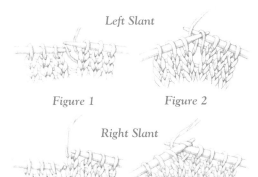

Figure 1   Figure 2

Right Slant

Figure 1   Figure 2

Unless otherwise indicated, work this increase as M1L.

Left Slant (M1L): With left needle tip, lift strand between needles from front to back (Figure 1). Knit the lifted loop through the back to twist the stitch (Figure 2).

Right Slant (M1R): With left needle tip, lift strand between needles from back to front (Figure 1). Knit the lifted loop through the front to twist the stitch (Figure 2).

Bar Increase (k1f&b)

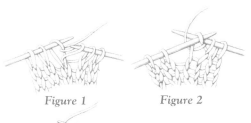

Figure 1   Figure 2

Figure 3

Knit into a stitch and leave it on the left needle (Figure 1), then knit through the back loop of the same stitch (Figure 2). There will be two stitches made from one (Figure 3).

Decreases

Ssk

Slip two stitches individually knitwise (Figure 1). Insert tip of left needle into front of these two slipped stitches and use right needle to knit them together through their back loops (Figure 2). (Some knitters like to slip the second stitch purlwise to make a more prominent decrease line.)

Figure 1   *Figure 2*

Centered Double Decrease

Slip two stitches together knitwise (Figure 1), knit the next stitch (Figure 2), then pass the two slipped stitches over the knitted stitch and off the needle (Figure 3).

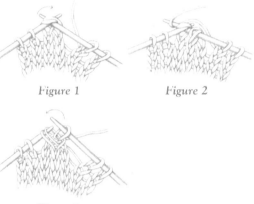

Figure 1   *Figure 2*

Figure 3

Bind Offs

Three-Needle Bind-Off

Place stitches to be joined onto two separate needles. Hold the needles so that right sides of knitting face together. *Insert a third needle into first stitch on each of the other two needles (Figure 1) and knit them together as one stitch (Figure 2), knit the next stitch on each needle together in the same way, then pass the first stitch over the second and off the needle (Figure 3). Repeat from * until one stitch remains on third needle. Cut yarn and pull tail through last stitch.

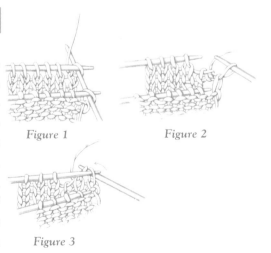

Figure 1   *Figure 2*

Figure 3

Suspended Bind-Off

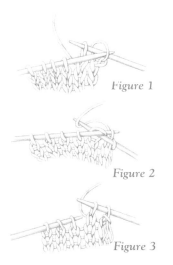

Figure 1

Figure 2

Figure 3

This method produces a very elastic edge. Slip one stitch, knit one stitch, *insert left needle tip into first stitch on right needle and lift the first stitch over the second (Figure 1). Leaving the first stitch on the left needle, knit the next stitch (Figure 2), then slip both stitches off the left needle—two stitches remain on right needle and one stitch has been bound off (Figure 3). Repeat from * until no stitches remain on left needle, then pass first stitch on right needle over the second.

Grafting

Kitchener Stitch

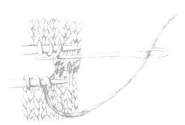

Place stitches to be joined onto two separate needles. Hold the needles parallel with points facing to the right and so that right sides of knitting are facing outward.

Step 1: Bring threaded needle through front stitch as if to purl and leave stitch on needle.

Step 2: Bring threaded needle through back stitch as if to knit and leave stitch on needle.

Step 3: Bring threaded needle through the same front stitch as if to knit and slip this stitch off needle. Bring threaded needle through next front stitch as if to purl and leave stitch on needle.

Step 4: Bring threaded needle through first back stitch as if to purl (as illustrated), slip that stitch off, bring needle through next back stitch as if to knit, leave this stitch on needle.

Repeat Steps 3 and 4 until no stitches remain on needle.

Pick Up and Knit

Along Bind-Off Edge

With right side facing and working from right to left, insert the tip of the needle into the center of the stitch below the bind-off edge (Figure 1), wrap yarn around needle, and pull it through (Figure 2). Pick up one stitch for every bound-off stitch.

Figure 1   *Figure 2*

Along Heel Gusset

With right side facing and working from right to left, insert tip of needle into the front half of chain-selvedge stitch (Figure 1) or into the entire chain-selvedge stitch (Figure 2), wrap yarn around needle, and pull it through. For a tighter join, pick up the stitches and knit them through the back loop (Figure 3). Pick up one stitch for every chain-selvedge stitch.

Figure 1   *Figure 2*

Figure 3

Along Shaped Edges

With right side facing and working from right to left, insert tip of needle between last and second-to-last stitches, wrap yarn around needle, and pull it through. Pick up and knit about three stitches for every four rows, adjusting as necessary so that the picked-up edge lays flat.

Crochet

Crochet Chain

Make a slipknot and place on crochet hook. *Yarn over hook and draw it through loop of the slipknot. Repeat from *, drawing yarn through loop on hook, for desired length. To fasten off, cut yarn and draw tail through last loop formed.

Single Crochet

Figure 1

Figure 2

*Insert crochet hook into a stitch, yarn over hook and draw a loop through stitch, yarn over hook again (Figure 1), and draw it through both loops on hook (Figure 2). Repeat from * for desired length.

Buttonholes

3 (4, 5) Stitch One-Row Buttonhole

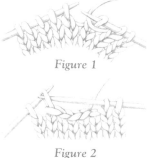

Figure 1

Figure 2

Figure 3

Figure 4

Work to where you want the buttonhole to begin, bring yarn to front, sl 1 pwise, bring yarn to back (Figure 1). *Sl 1 pwise, pass first slipped st over second; rep from * 2 (3, 4) more times. Place last st back on left needle (Figure 2), turn. CO 4 (5, 6) sts as follows: *Insert right needle between the first and second sts on left needle, draw up a loop, and place it on the left needle (Figure 3); rep from * 3 (4, 5) more times, turn. Bring yarn to back, slip first st of left needle onto right needle and pass last CO st over it (Figure 4), work to end of row.

I-Cord

Standard

With double-pointed needle, cast on desired number of stitches (three stitches shown here). *Without turning the needle, slide the stitches to the other point, pull yarn around the back, and knit the stitches as usual. Repeat from * for desired length.

Attached

As I-cord is knitted, attach it to the garment as follows: With right side of garment facing and using a separate ball of yarn and circular needle, pick up the desired number of stitches along the garment edge. Slide these stitches down the needle so that the first picked-up stitch is near the opposite needle point. With double-pointed needle, cast on desired number of I-cord stitches. Knit across the I-cord to the last stitch, then knit the last stitch together with the first picked-up stitch on the garment. *Pull the yarn behind the cord, knit to the last I-cord stitch, then knit the last I-cord stitch together with the next picked-up stitch. Repeat from * until all picked-up stitches have been used.

Embellishments

Pompom

Figure 1

Figure 2

Figure 3

Cut two circles of cardboard, each ½" (1.3 cm) larger than desired finished pompom width. Cut a small circle out of the center and a small edge out of the side of each circle (Figure 1). Tie a strand of yarn between the circles, hold circles together and wrap with yarn—the more wraps, the thicker the pompom. Cut between the circles and knot the tie strand tightly (Figure 2). Place pompom between two smaller cardboard circles held together with a needle and trim the edges (Figure 3). This technique comes from *Nicky Epstein's Knitted Embellishments*, Interweave Press, 1999.

Tassel

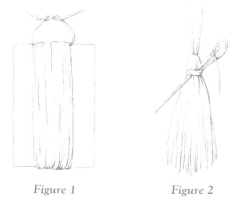

Figure 1   *Figure 2*

Cut a piece of cardboard 4" (10 cm) wide by the desired length of the tassel plus 1" (2.5 cm). Wrap yarn to desired thickness around cardboard. Cut a short length of yarn and tie tightly around one end of wrapped yarn (Figure 1). Cut yarn loops at other end. Cut another piece of yarn and wrap tightly around loops a short distance below top knot to form tasssel neck. Knot securely, thread ends onto tapestry needle, and pull to center of tassel (Figure 2). Trim ends.

beg	begin; begins; beginning
bet	between
BO	bind off
cm	centimeter(s)
CO	cast on
cont	continue(s); continuing
dec(s)	decrease(s); decreasing
dpn	double-pointed needles(s)
foll	follows; following
g	gram(s)
inc	increase(s); increasing
k	knit
k1f&b	knit into front and back of same stitch (increase)
k2tog	knit two stitches together (decrease)
kwise	knitwise
m(s)	marker(s)
mm	millimeter(s)
M1	make one (increase)
p	purl
p1f&b	purl into front and back of same stitch (increase)
p2tog	purl two stitches together (decrease)
patt(s)	pattern(s)
pm	place marker
psso	pass slipped stitch over stitch just knitted
p2sso	pass 2 slipped stitches over stitch just knitted
pwise	purlwise
rem	remain(s); remaining
rep	repeat; repeating
rev St st	reverse stockinette stitch
rnd(s)	round(s)
RS	right side
sl	slip (slip stitch purlwise unless otherwise indicated)
sl st	slip(ped) stitch
ssk	slip two stitches individually knitwise, knit the two slipped stitches together through the back loops (decrease)
st(s)	stitch(es)
tbl	through back loop
tog	together
WS	wrong side
yo	yarnover
*	repeat starting point (i.e., repeat from *)
( )	alternate measurements and/or instructions
[ ]	instructions that are to be worked as a group a specified number of times

yarnsources

The following companies supplied yarn for the projects photographed in this book.

Baabajoes Wool vests
PO Box 260604
Lakewood, CO 80226
www.baabajoeswool.com
- NZ WoolPak 12-Ply (100% wool; 310 yd [283 m]/250 g)
- NZ WoolPak 10-Ply (100% wool; 430 yd [393 m]/250 g)
- NZ WoolPak 8-Ply (100% wool; 525 yd [480 m]/250 g)

Brown Sheep Company mittens
100662 County Rd. 16
Mitchell, NE 69357
www.brownsheep.com
- Handpaint Originals (70% mohair, 30% wool; 88 yd [80 m]/50 g)
- Nature Spun Worsted (100% wool; 245 yd [224 m]/100 g)
- Top of the Lamb Sport (100% wool; 154 yd [141 m]/50 g)
- Nature Spun Fingering (100% wool; 310 yd [283 m]/50 g)

Classic Elite Yarns sweaters
300 Jackson St.
Lowell, MA 01852
- Gatsby (70% wool, 15% viscose, 15% nylon; 94 yd [86 m]/100 g)
- Montera (50% llama, 50% wool; 127 yd [116 m]/100 g)
- Waterspun (100% Merino; 138 yd [123 m]/50 g)

Dale of Norway tams
N16 W23390 Stoneridge Dr., Ste. A
Waukesha, WI 53188
www.dale.no
- Free Style (100% wool; 87 yd [80 m]/50 g)
- Falk (100% wool; 116 yd [106 m]/50 g)
- Daletta (100% wool; 154 yd [141 m]/50 g)
- Baby Ull (100% wool; 191 yd [175 m]/50 g)

GGH/Muench Yarns scarves
285 Bel Marin Keys Blvd., Unit J
Novato, CA 94949-5724
- Lamour (50% wool, 33% angora, 17% nylon; 88 yd [80 m]/25 g)
- Soft Kid (70% super kid mohair 25% polyamid, 5% wool; 151 yd [138 m]/25 g)
- Merino Soft (100% Merino; 186 yd [170 m]/50 g)

Lane Borgosesia hats
527 South Tejon, Ste. 200
Colorado Springs, CO 80903
- KnitUSA (100% wool; 110 yd [100 m]/100 g)
- Knitaly (100% wool; 215 yd [196 m]/100 g)
- Aerobic (100% Merino; 180 yd [165 m]/50 g)
- Merinos Extra Fine (100% Merino; 185 yd [170 m]/50 g)

Needful Yarns gloves
156 Royal Palm Dr.
Thornhill, ON L4J 8K1
Canada
better.future@sympatico.ca
- Super (100% Merino; 128 yd [117 m]/100 g)
- Extra (100% Merino; 99 yd [90 m]/50 g)
- Australian Merino (100% Merino; 153 yd [140 m]/50 g)

Plymouth Yarn Company socks
PO Box 28
Bristol, PA 19007
www.plymouthyarn.com
- Galway Highland Heather (100% wool; 210 yd [192 m]/100 g)
- La Fibre Nobili Merino Superfine (100% virgin wool; 172 yd [158 m]/50 g)
- Filati Bertagna Gaia (100% extra fine Merino; 110 yd [100 m]/50 g)

acknowledgments

Although my name appears on the cover, making this book was not an individual effort. It is the culmination of the help, encouragement, and inspiration of many family members, friends, and colleagues, as well as every knitter whose path I've crossed. Foremost, I must thank my parents, Barbara and Ted Walker. In 1968 they took me to Switzerland during my father's sabbatical and enrolled me in public school, where I learned the craft that has become such an integral part of my life. I am grateful to my colleagues at Interweave Press, and especially *Interweave Knits*®, who have done so much for me, both professionally and personally. In particular, I'd like to mention Melanie Falick, editor extraordinaire, friend, and mentor, who pushed me beyond my comfort zone, yet never doubted my ability to bring it all together. I am also indebted to Lori Gayle for her keen technical eye and ability to make sense of all the numbers; to Leigh Radford for designing pages that are clear, unintimidating, and beautiful—a daunting task given the academic nature of the text; to Gayle Ford for the technical illustrations in the Glossary; to Paulette Livers for illustrating the many variations of edgings and finishings; and to Priscilla Gibson-Roberts for her insight on tam shaping and sock sizing and Shirley Paden for sharing her formula for shaping sleeve caps. A special thank you goes to all the companies who donated the yarn for the projects shown in the photographs, and to Lynn Gates for knitting two of the vests. Most of all, I would like to thank my husband, David, and our three boys, Alex, Eric, and Nicholas, for accepting my passion for knitting, even when it borders on the compulsive. Last, but not least, I wish to thank publisher Linda Ligon for her support throughout this project and for her role in promoting knitting in general.

index

personalknittingnotes

MEASUREMENTS AND OTHER IMPORTANT DETAILS

personalknittingnotes